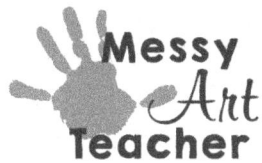

Messy Art Teacher Sites

For free art lesson ideas and tips visit
messyartteacher.wordpress.com
or video art tips
youtube.com/messyartteacher

Copyright © 2020 by Messy Art Teacher.

All rights reserved. No part of this publication may be reproduced, distributed, or transmitted in any form or by any means, including photocopying, recording, or other electronic or mechanical methods, without the prior written permission of the publisher, except in the case of brief quotations embodied in critical reviews and certain other noncommercial uses permitted by copyright law. For permission requests, write to the publisher, addressed "Attention: Permissions Coordinator," at the address below.

Messy Art Teacher Press
PO Box 2844
Richmond Hill, GA 31324

Copyright © 2020 by Messy Art Teacher. All rights reserved.

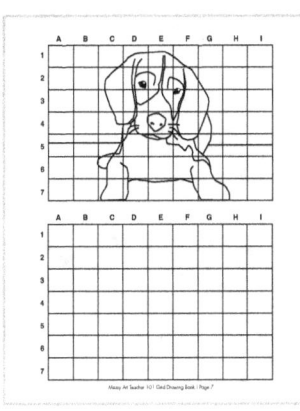
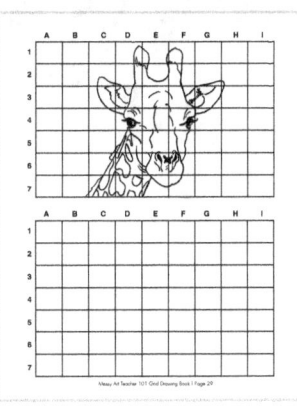
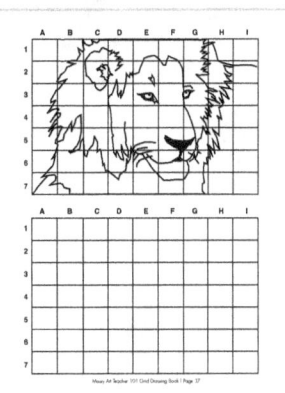
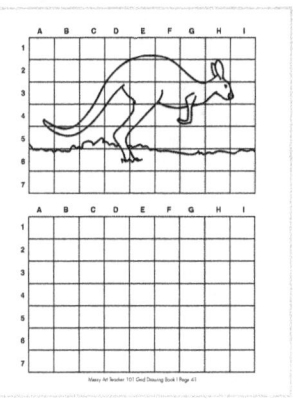

This book belongs to

_____

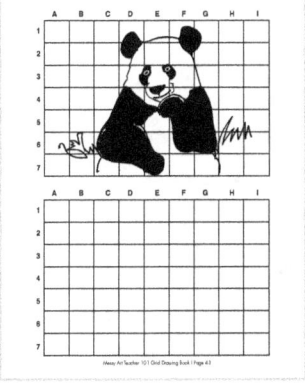
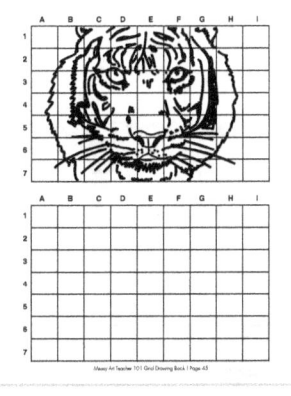
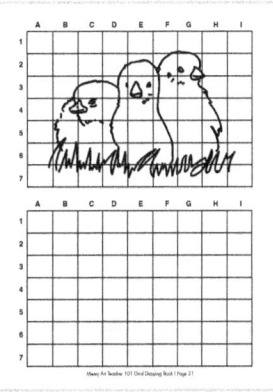
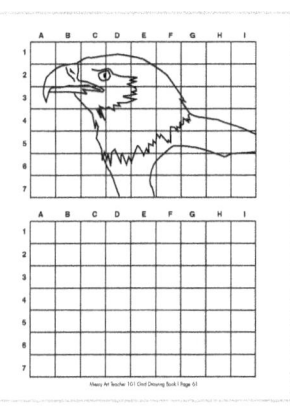

Directions

Recreate the drawing in the bottom grid. The letters and numbers on the side of the grid act as coordinates, so you can find the same square. Look at the top grid and find the square that you want to start with.

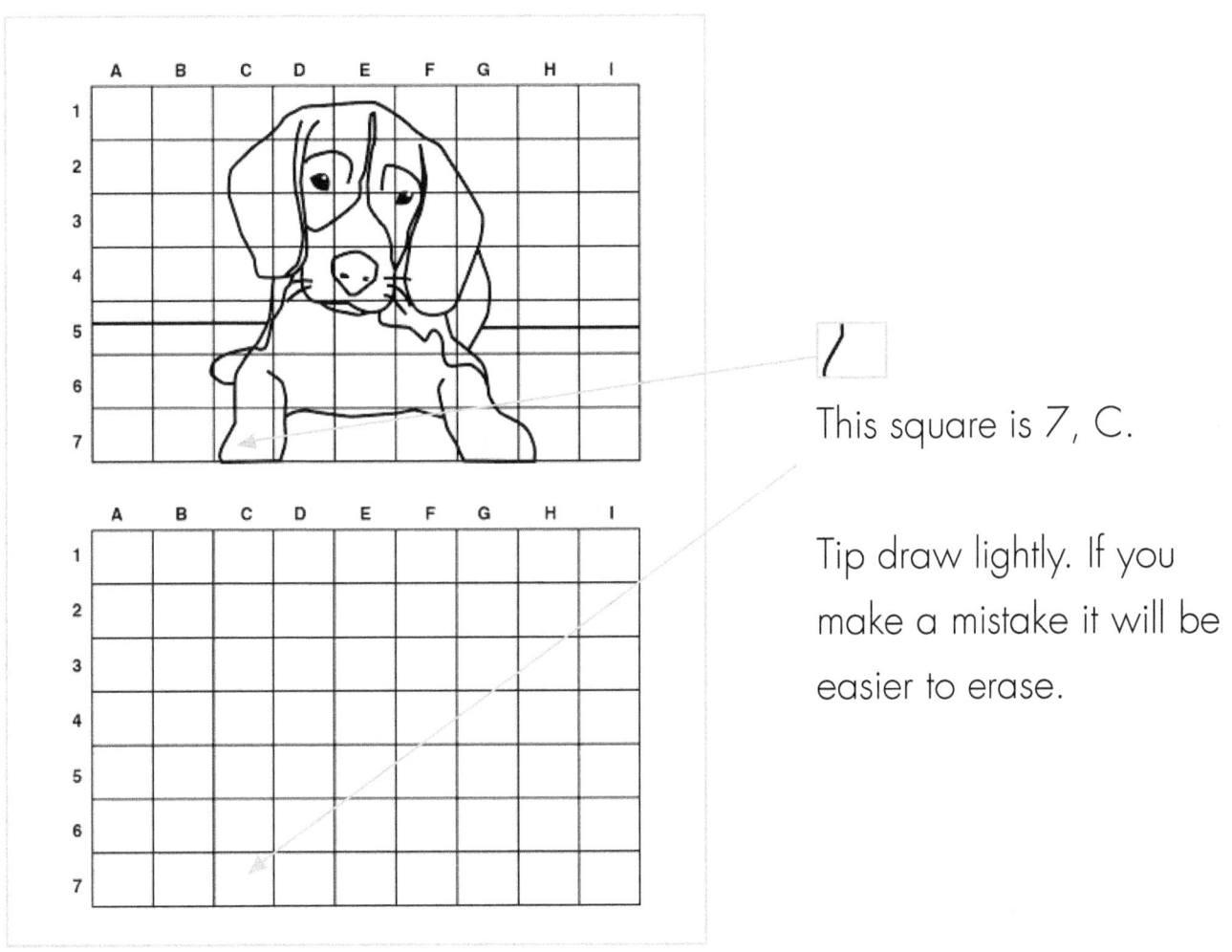

This square is 7, C.

Tip draw lightly. If you make a mistake it will be easier to erase.

Drawing on a grid makes it easier to break down a complex image into smaller parts. Draw with a pencil, and when you finish you can color it in. Take a photo of your finished grid drawing and share with the world.

Bonus page 93 Make your own grid drawing sheet and challenge a friend!

Copyright © 2020 by Messy Art Teacher. All rights reserved.

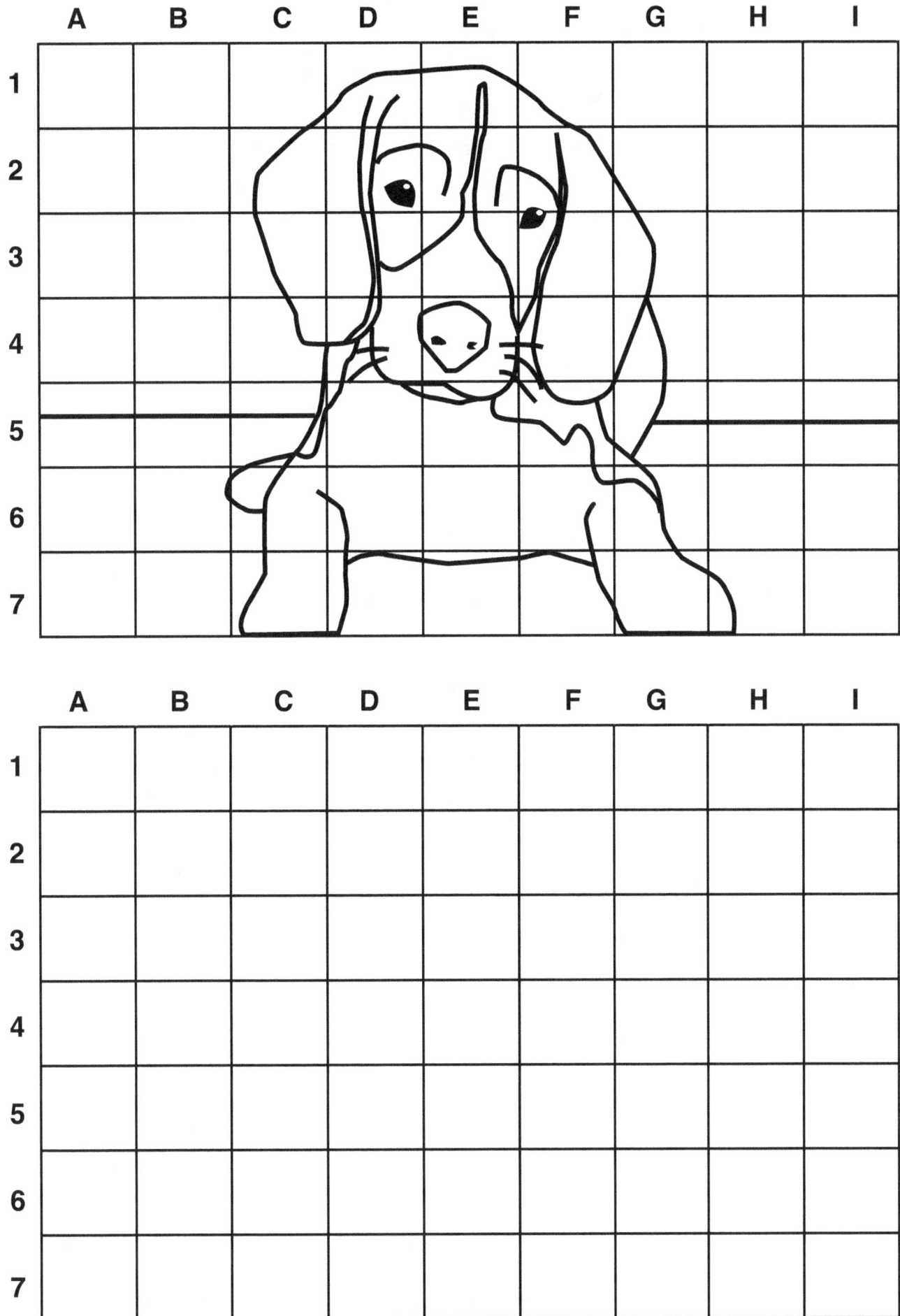

Messy Art Teacher 101 Grid Drawing Book | Page 7

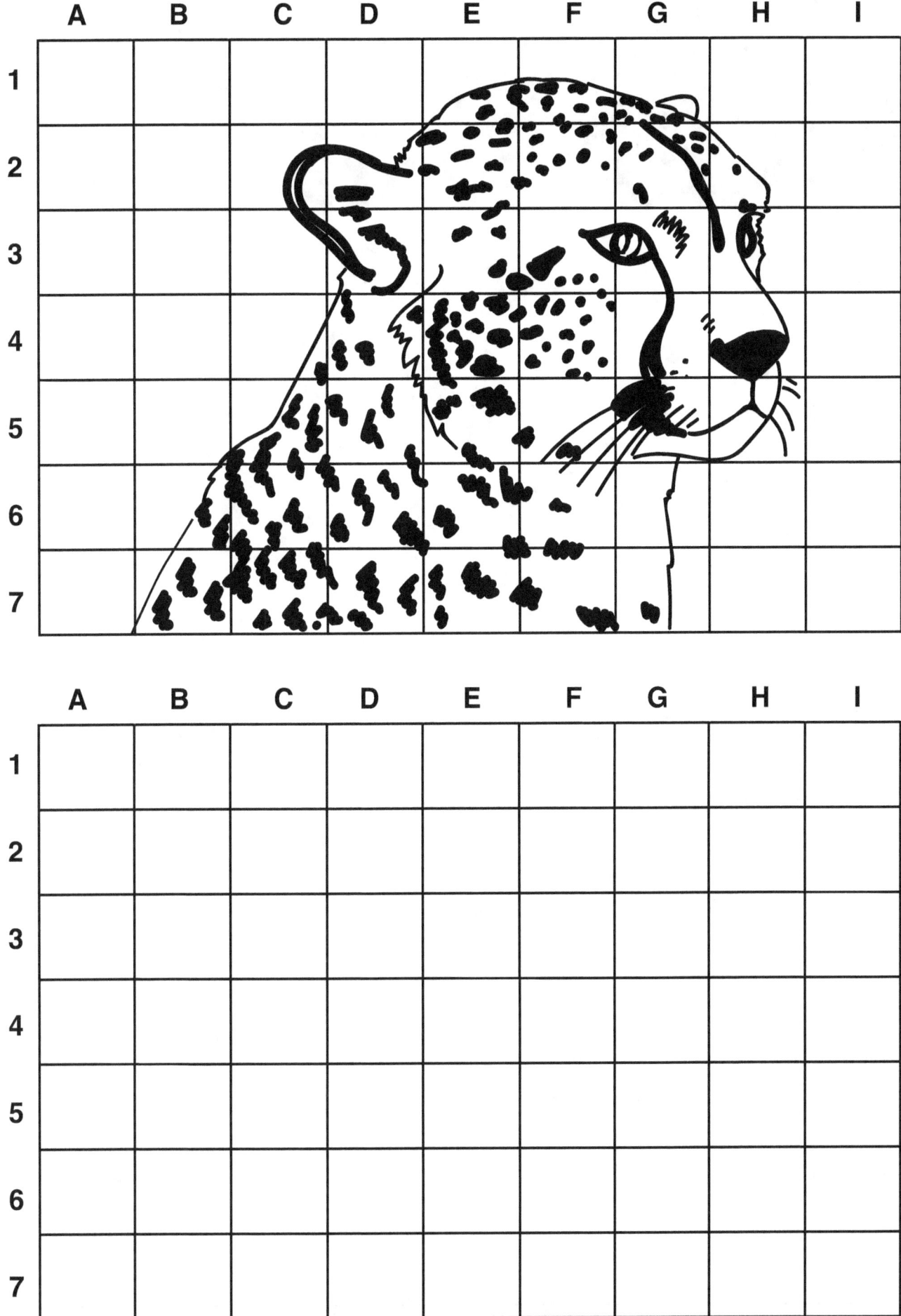

Copyright © 2020 by Messy Art Teacher. All rights reserved.

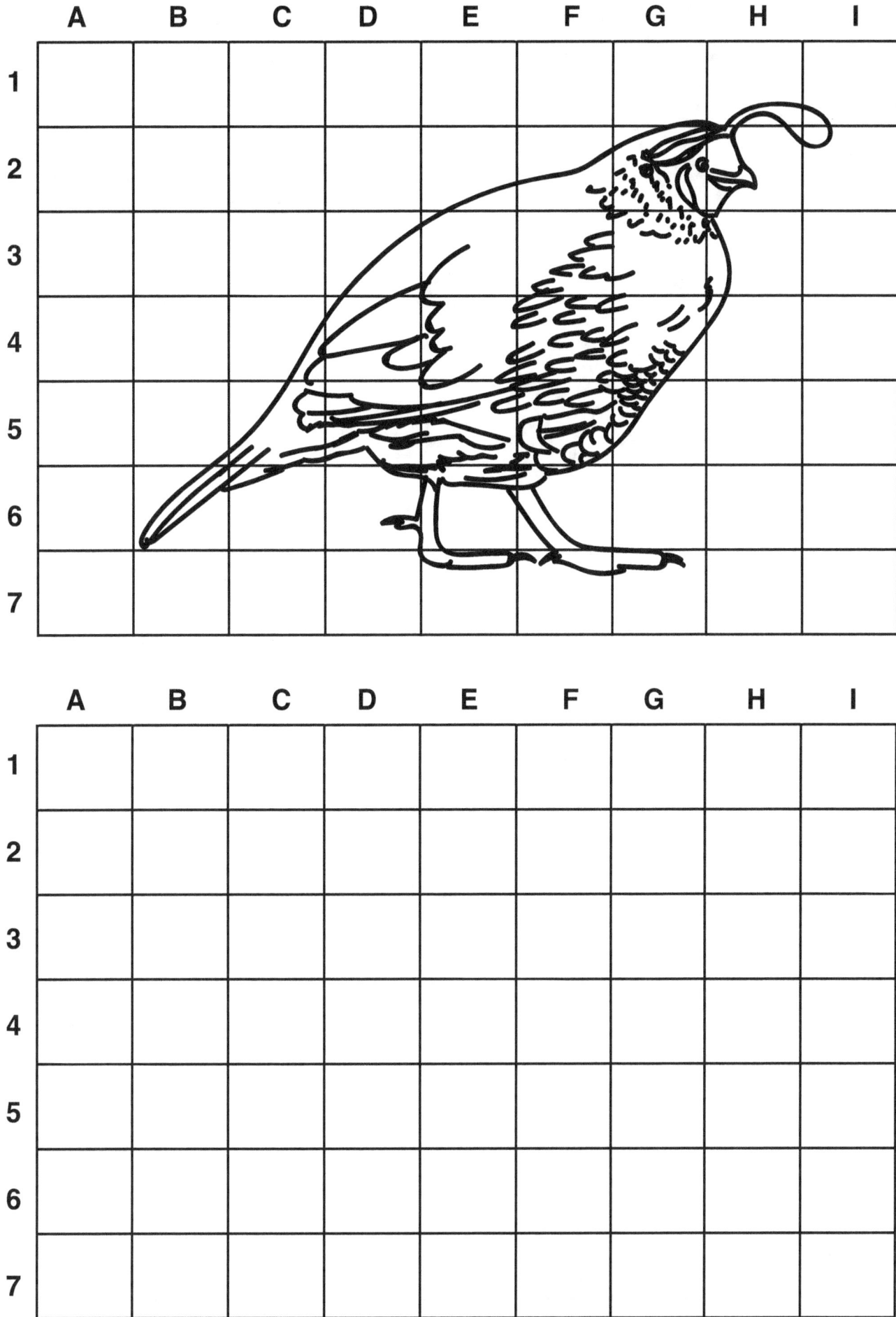

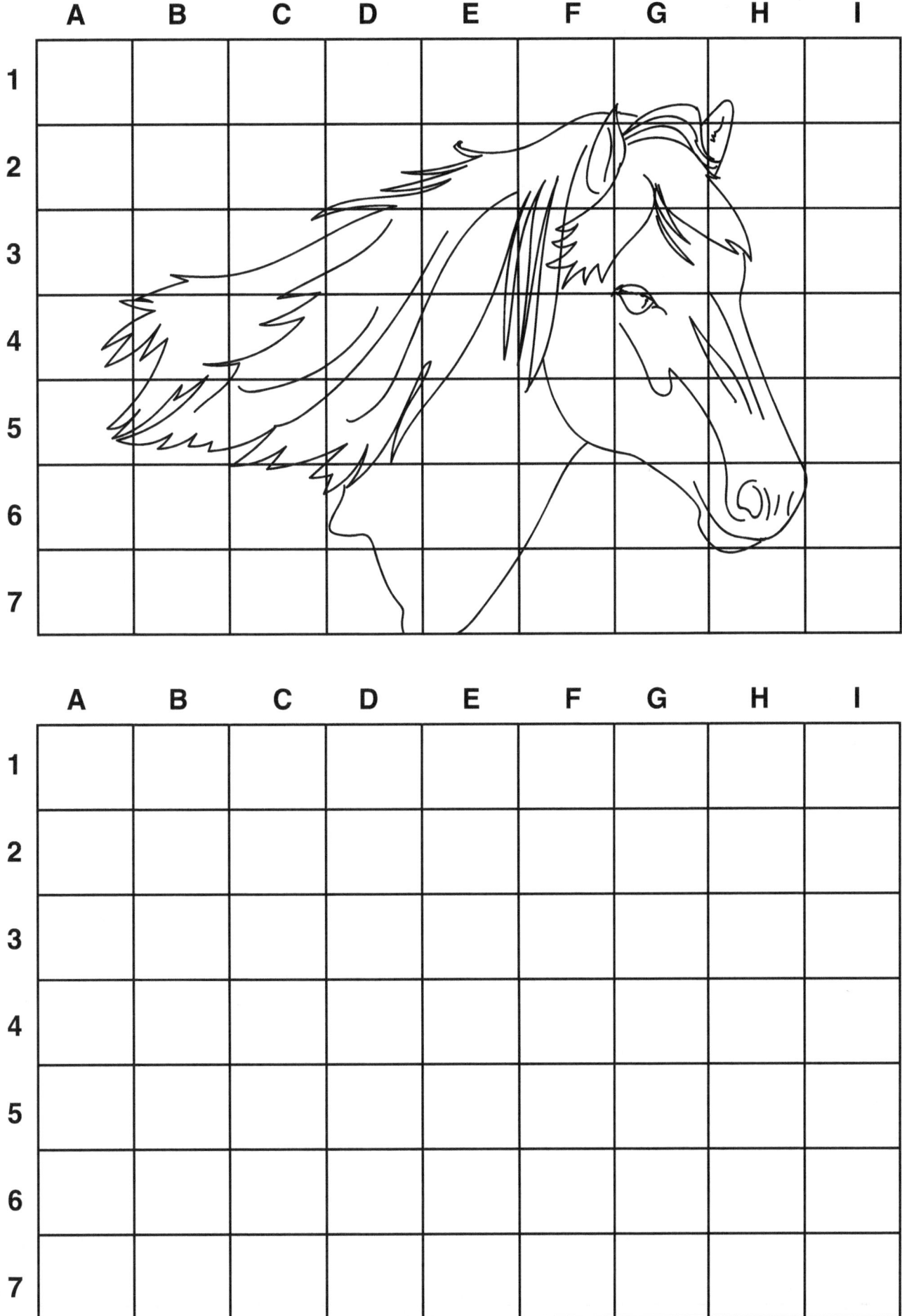

Copyright © 2020 by Messy Art Teacher. All rights reserved.

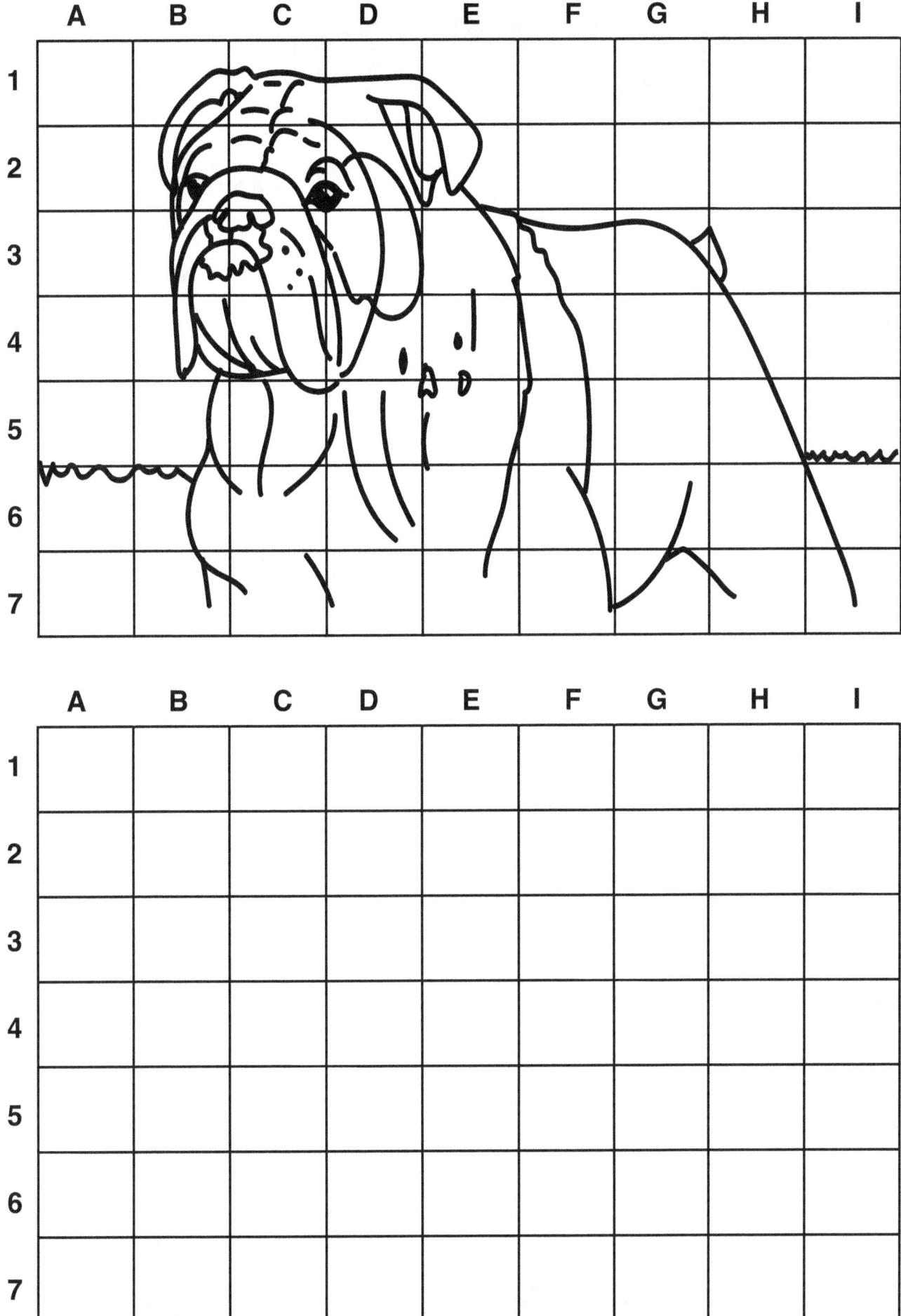

Messy Art Teacher 101 Grid Drawing Book | Page 15

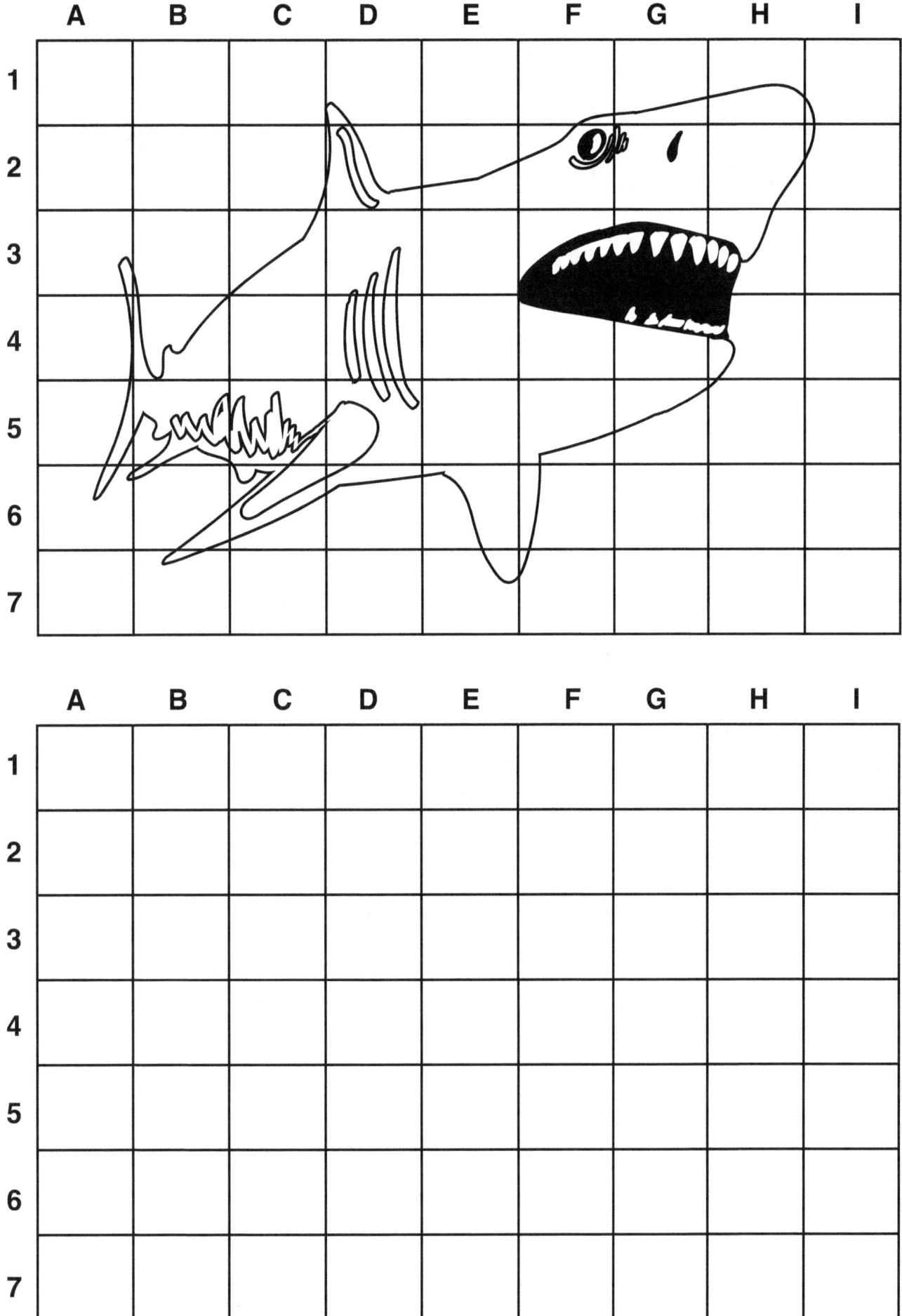

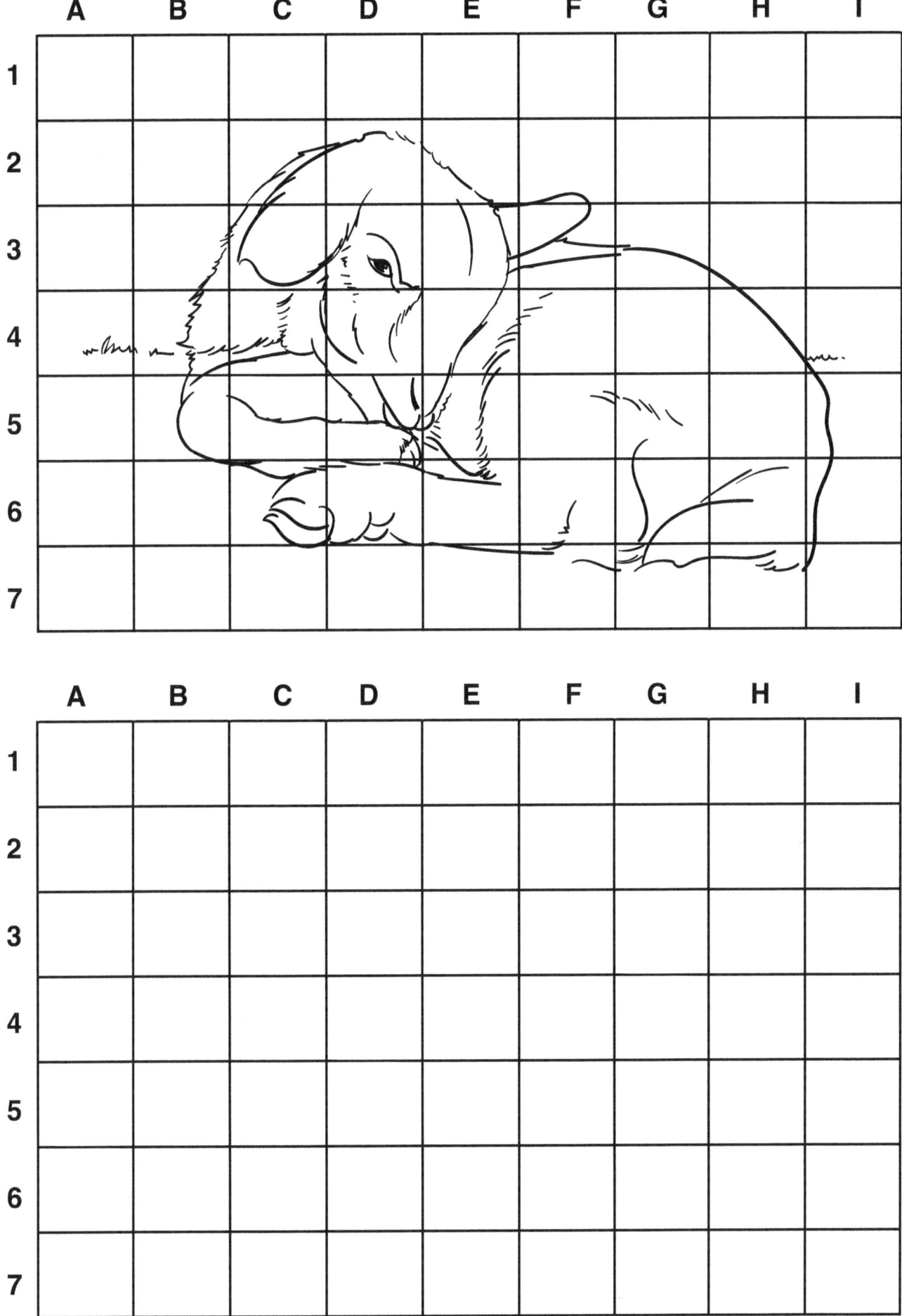

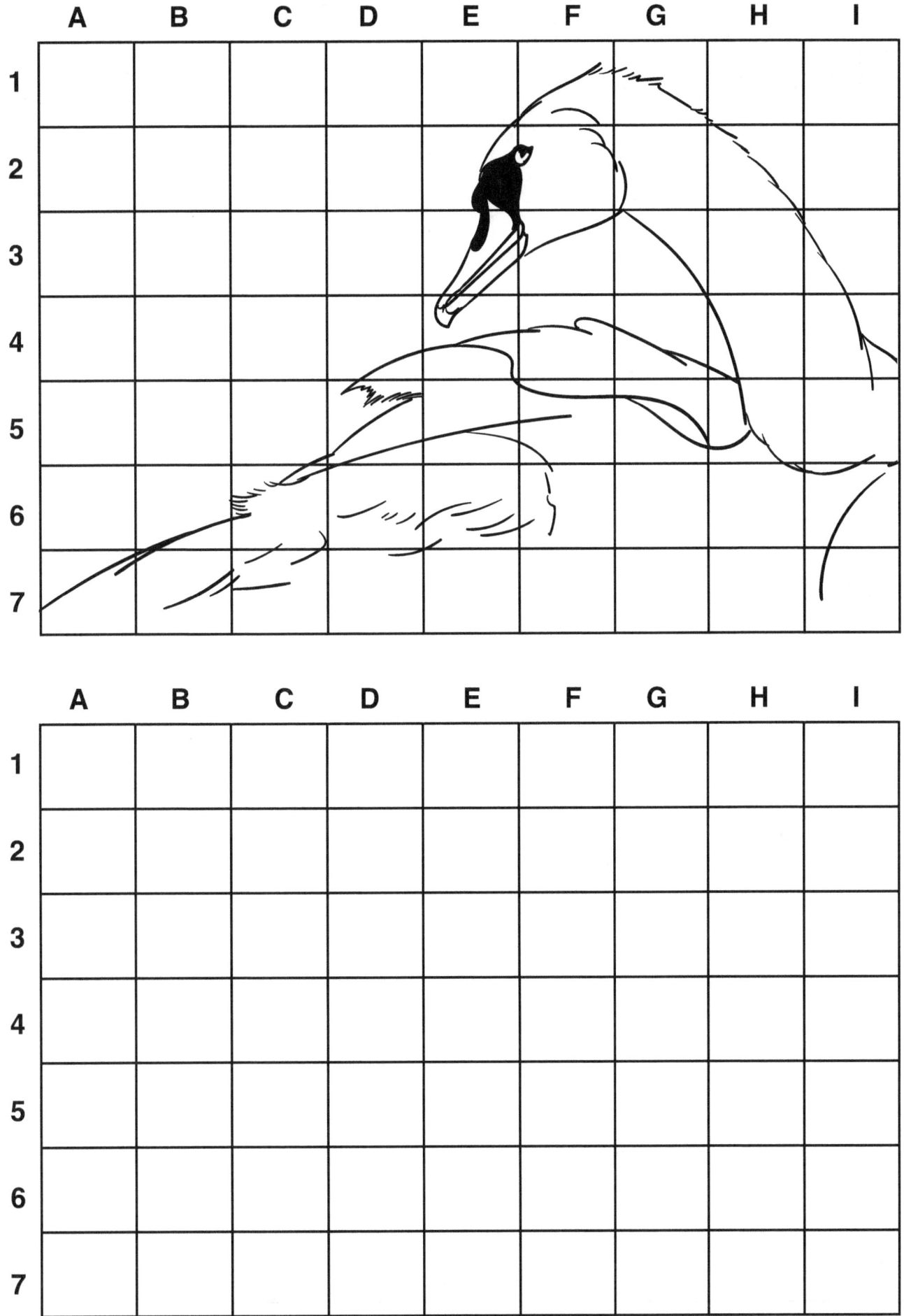

Messy Art Teacher 101 Grid Drawing Book | Page 21

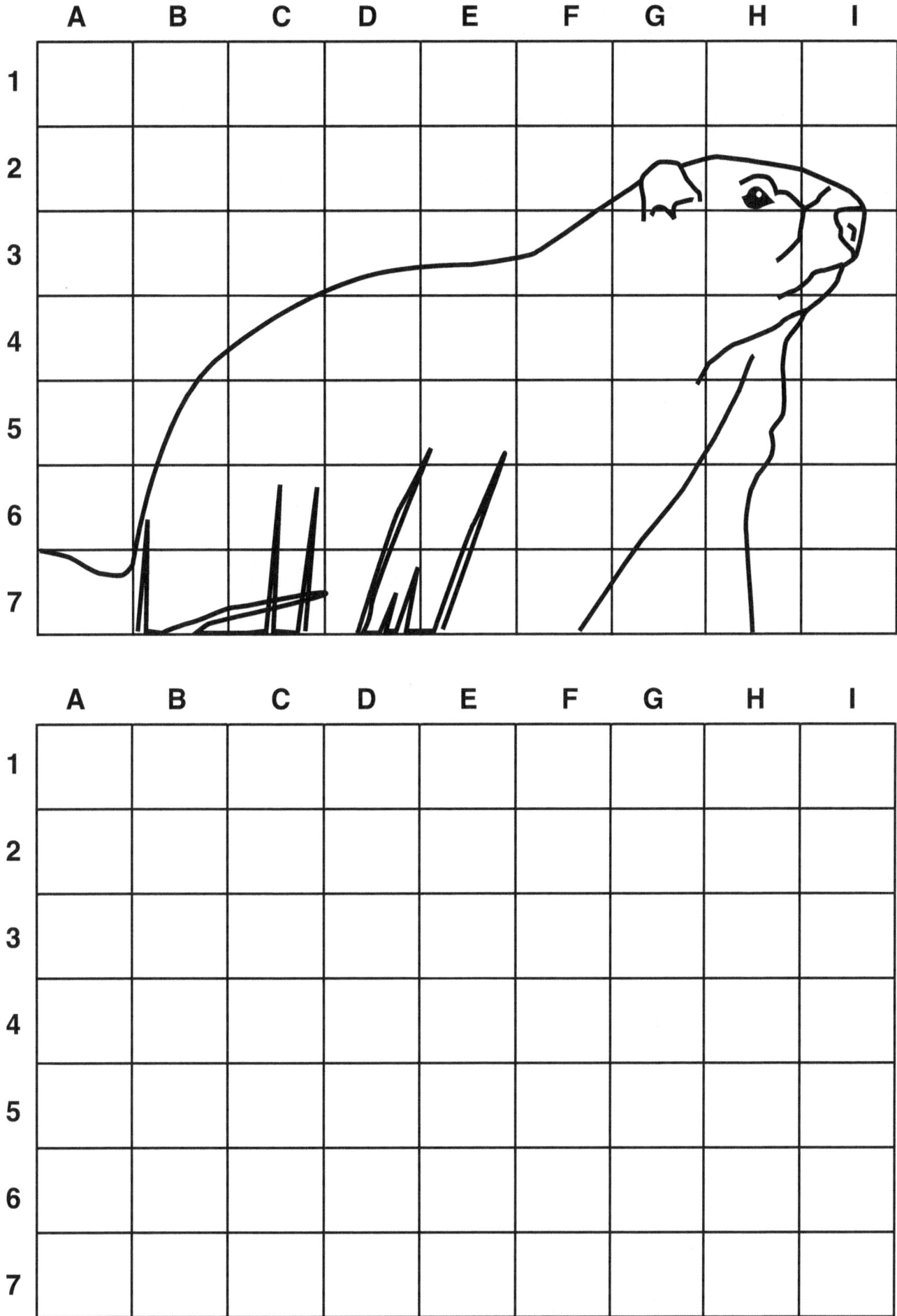

Copyright © 2020 by Messy Art Teacher. All rights reserved.

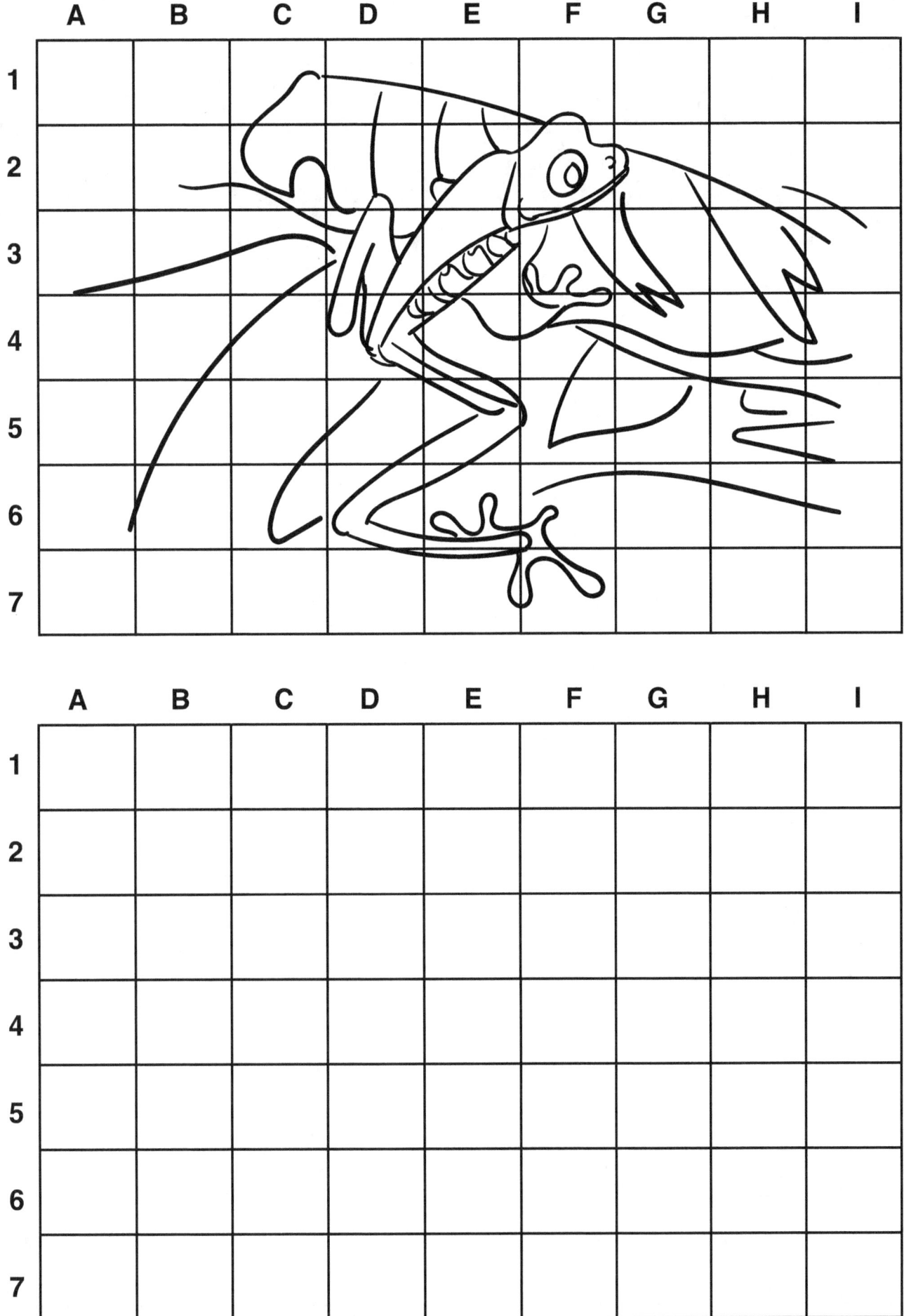

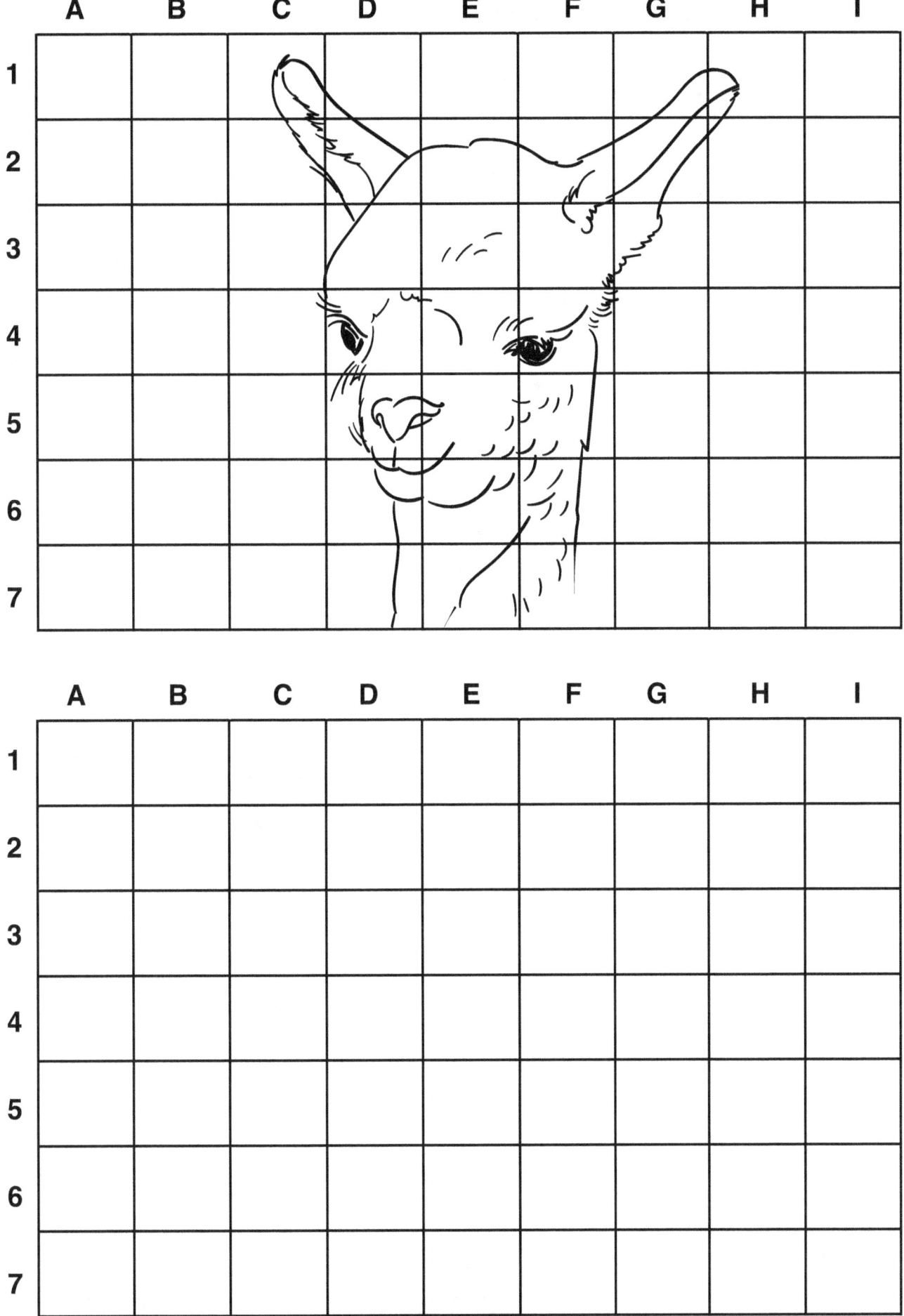

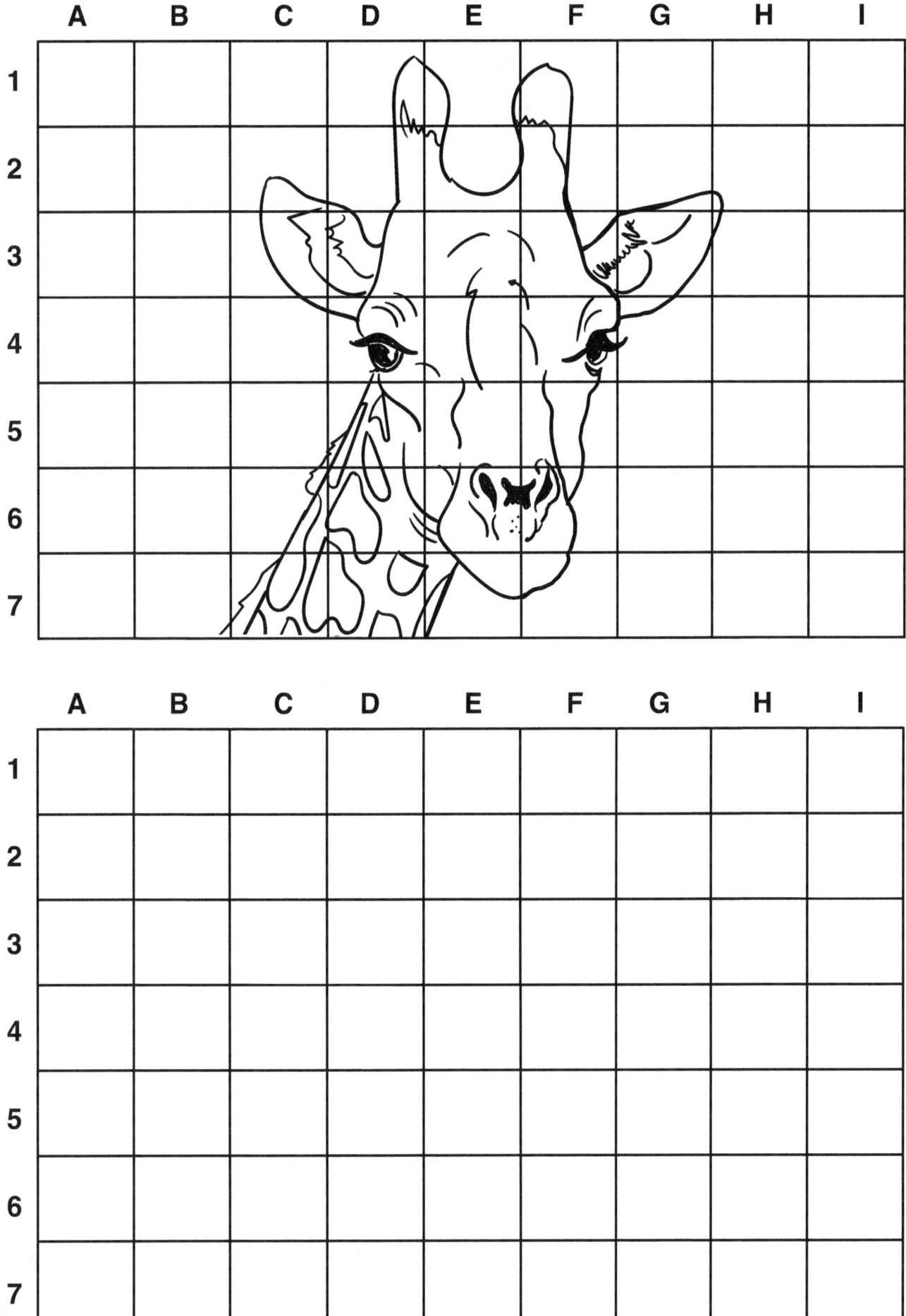

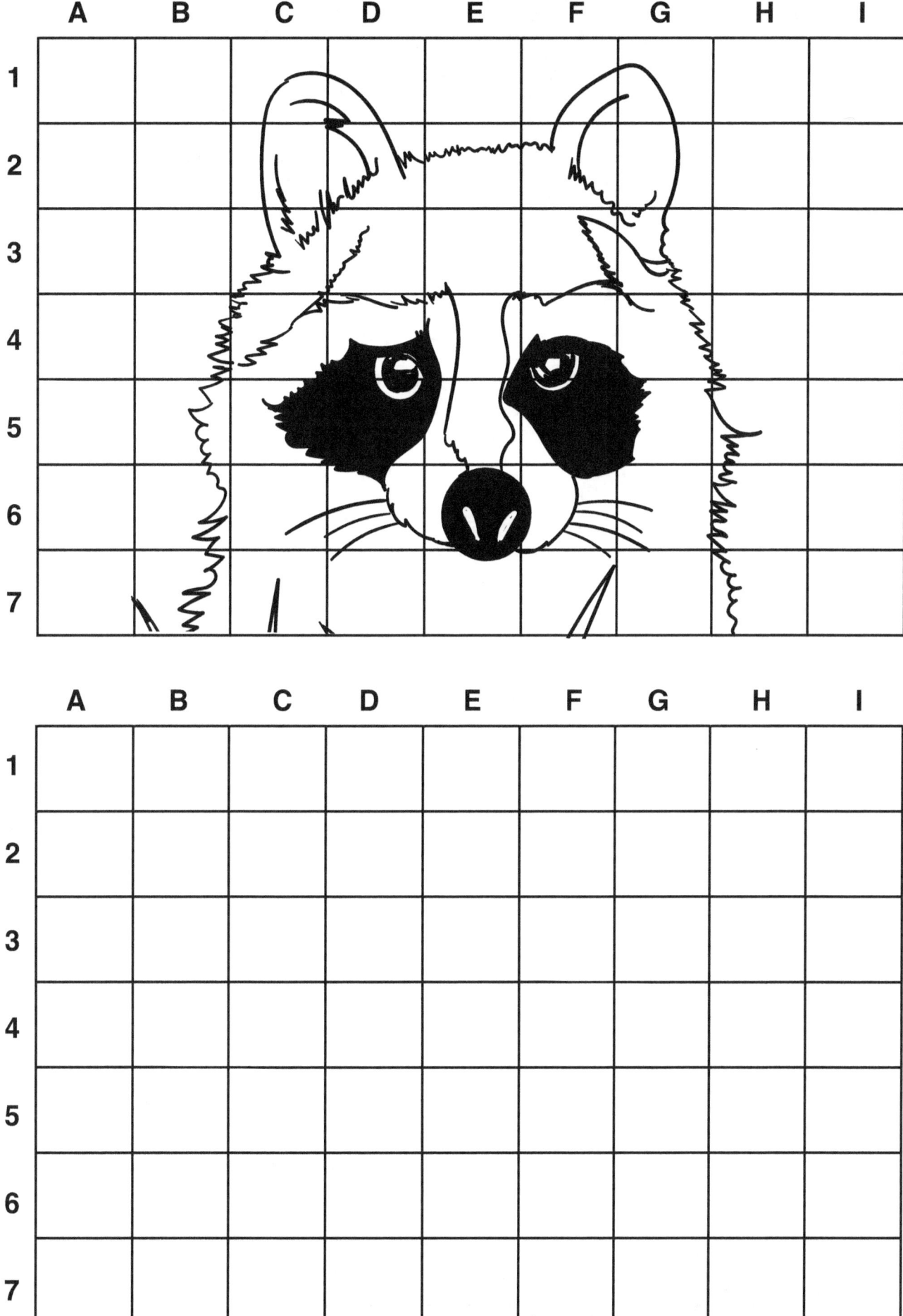

Messy Art Teacher 101 Grid Drawing Book | Page 31

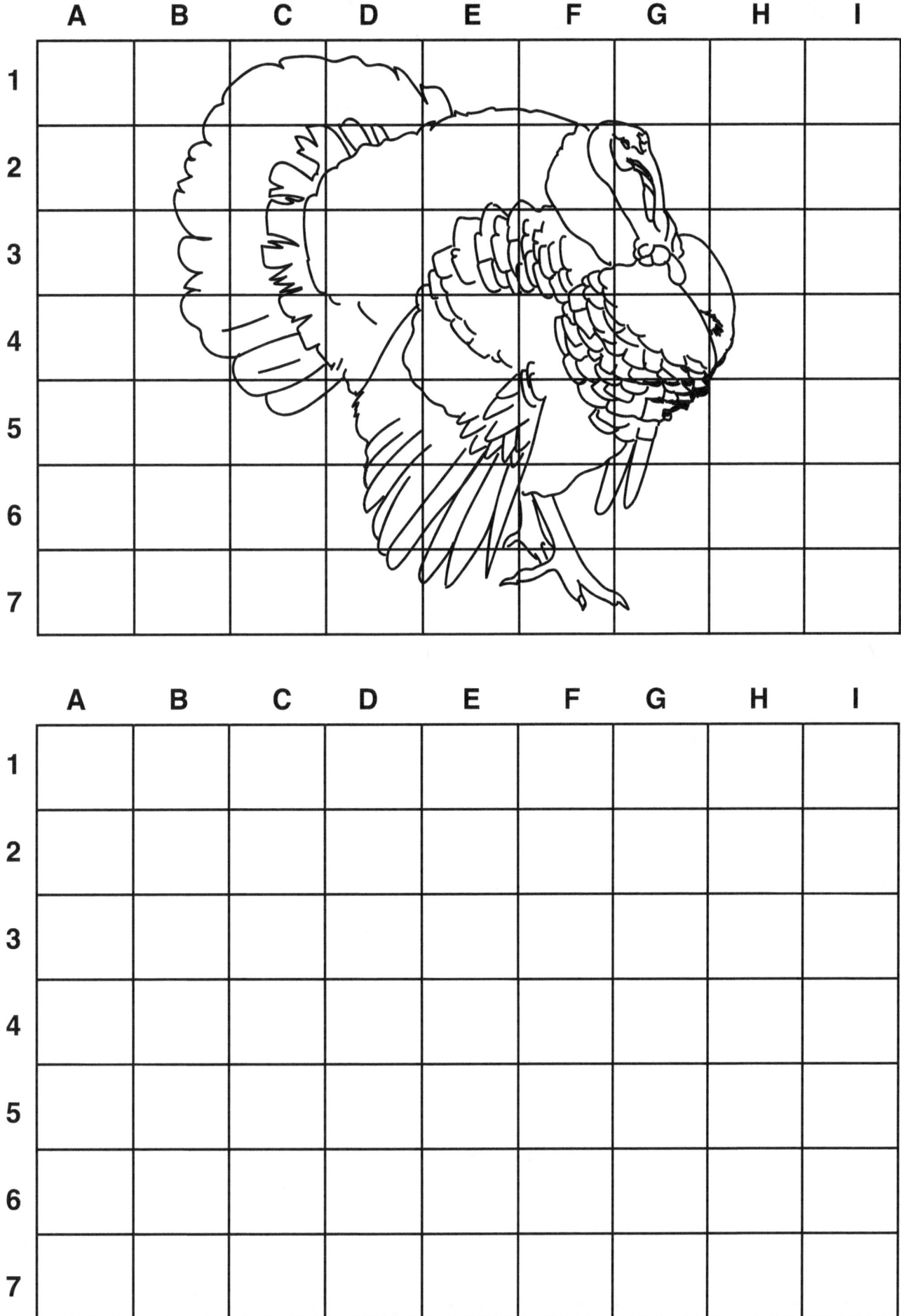

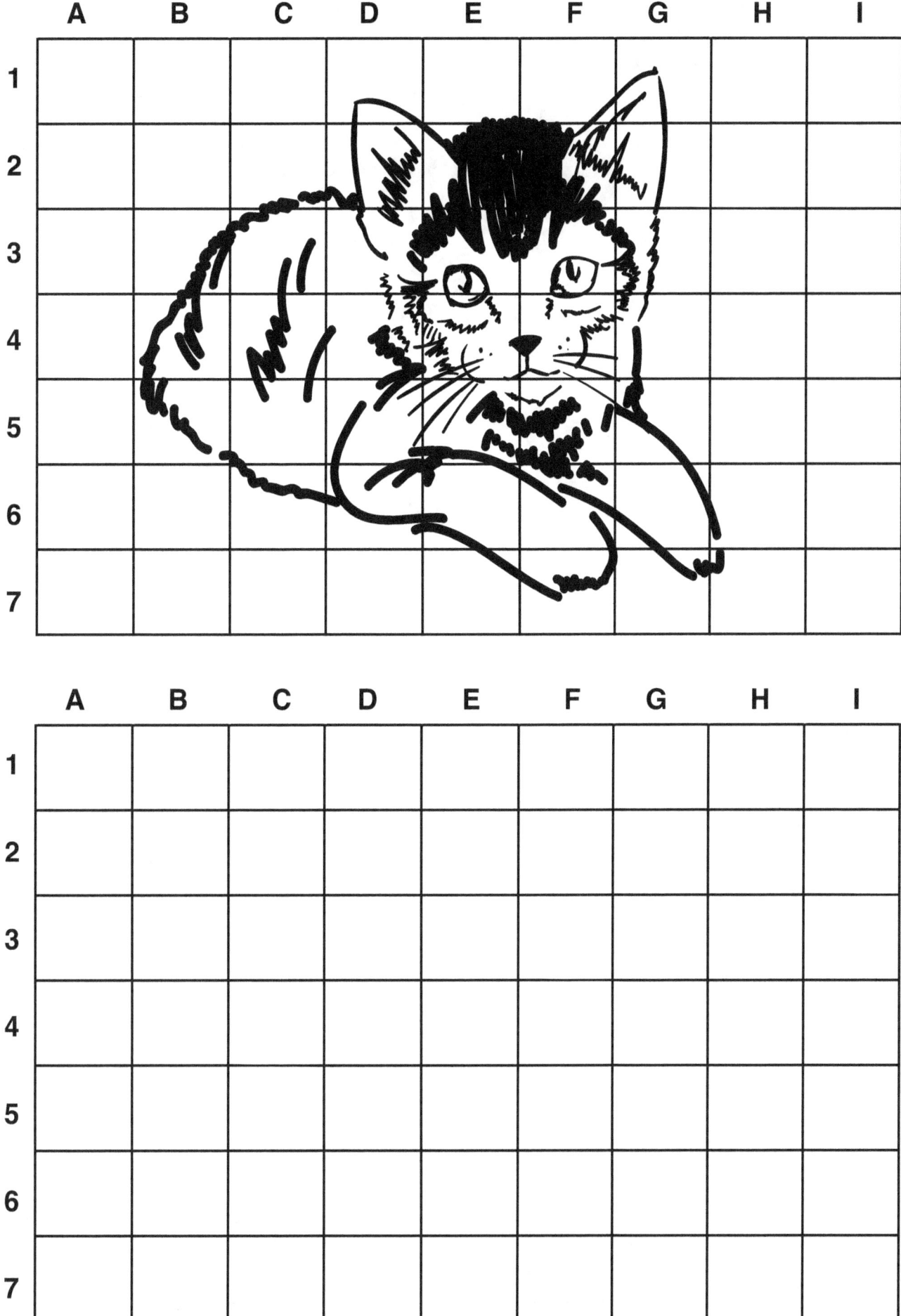

Messy Art Teacher 101 Grid Drawing Book | Page 35

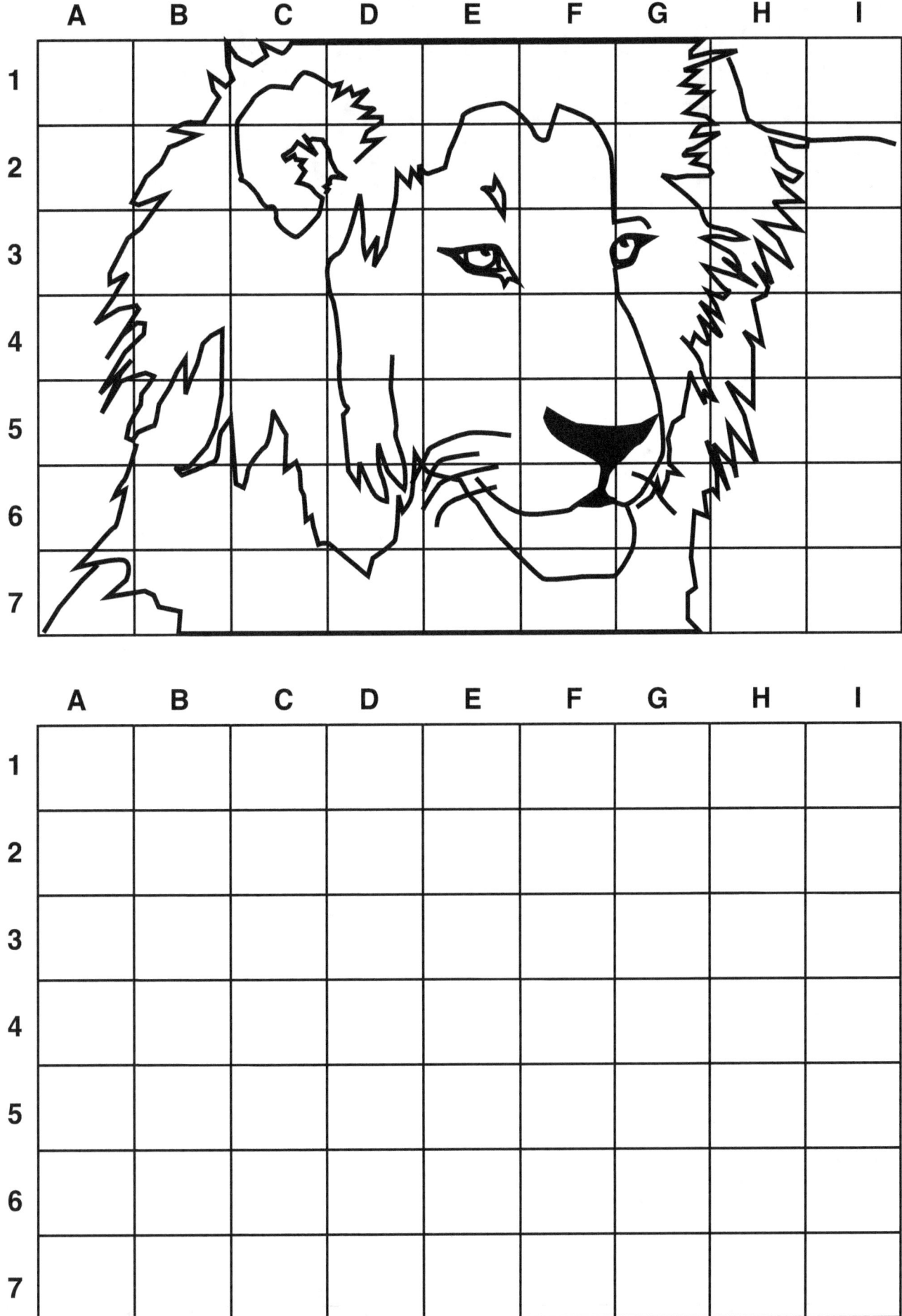

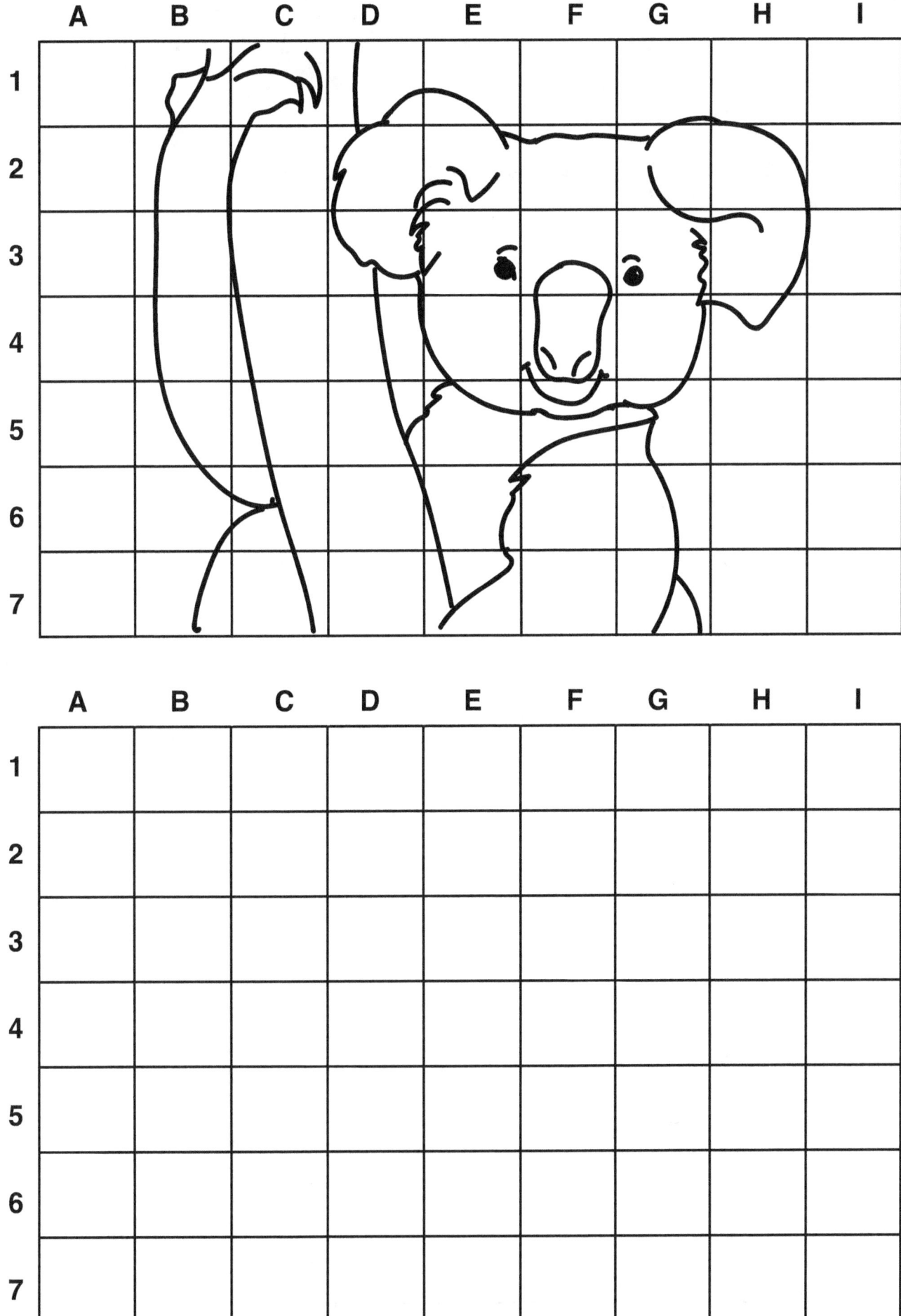

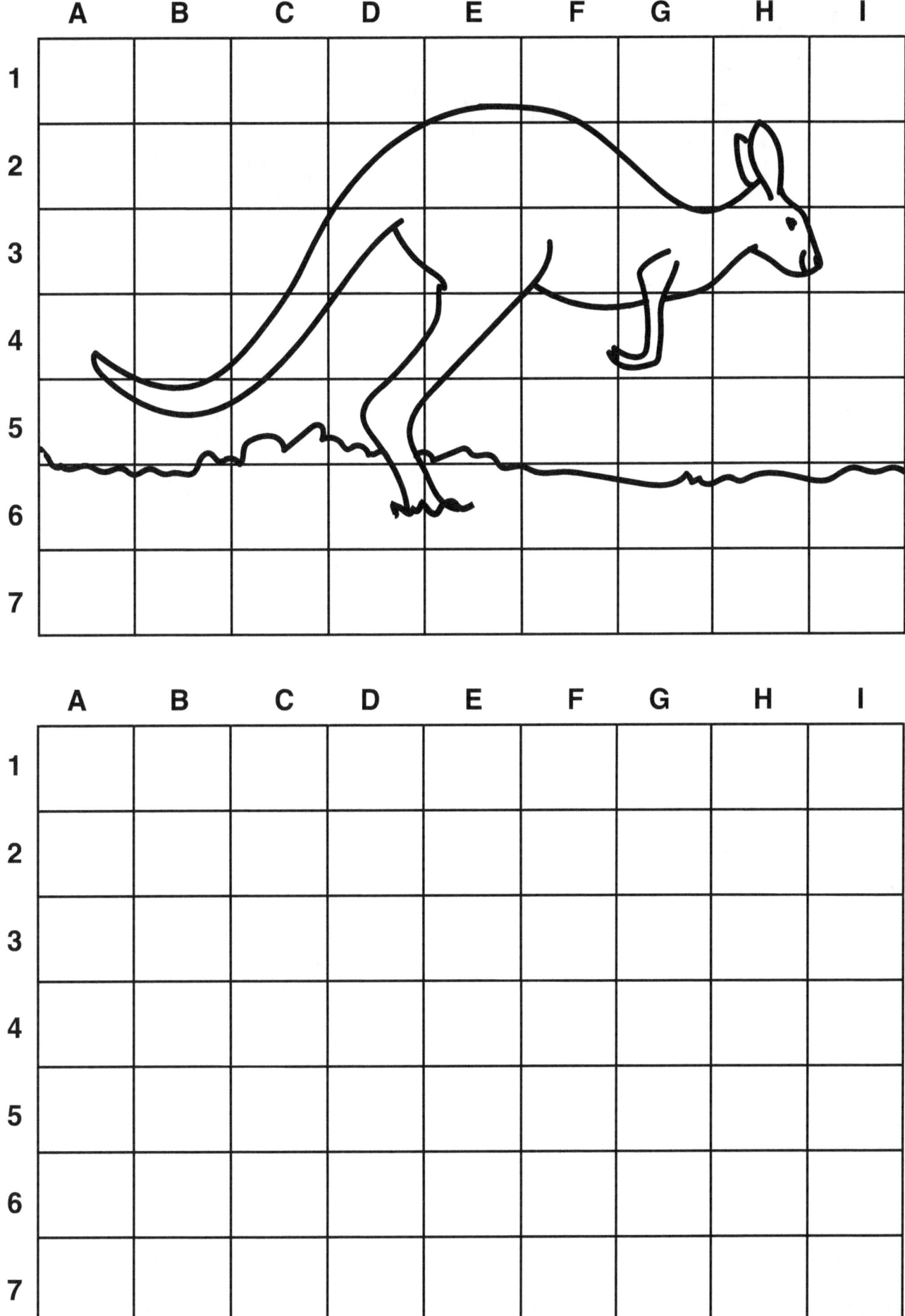

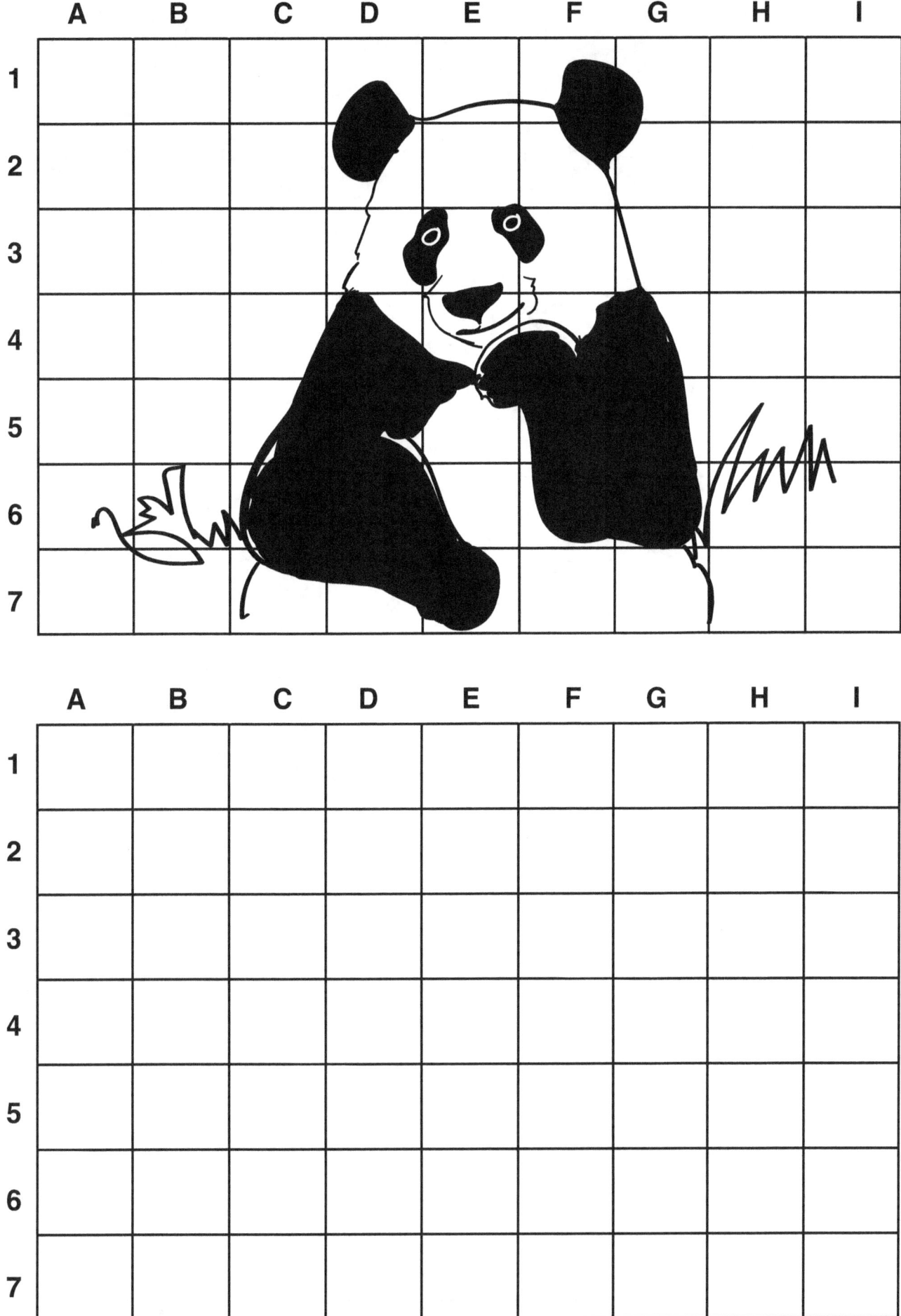

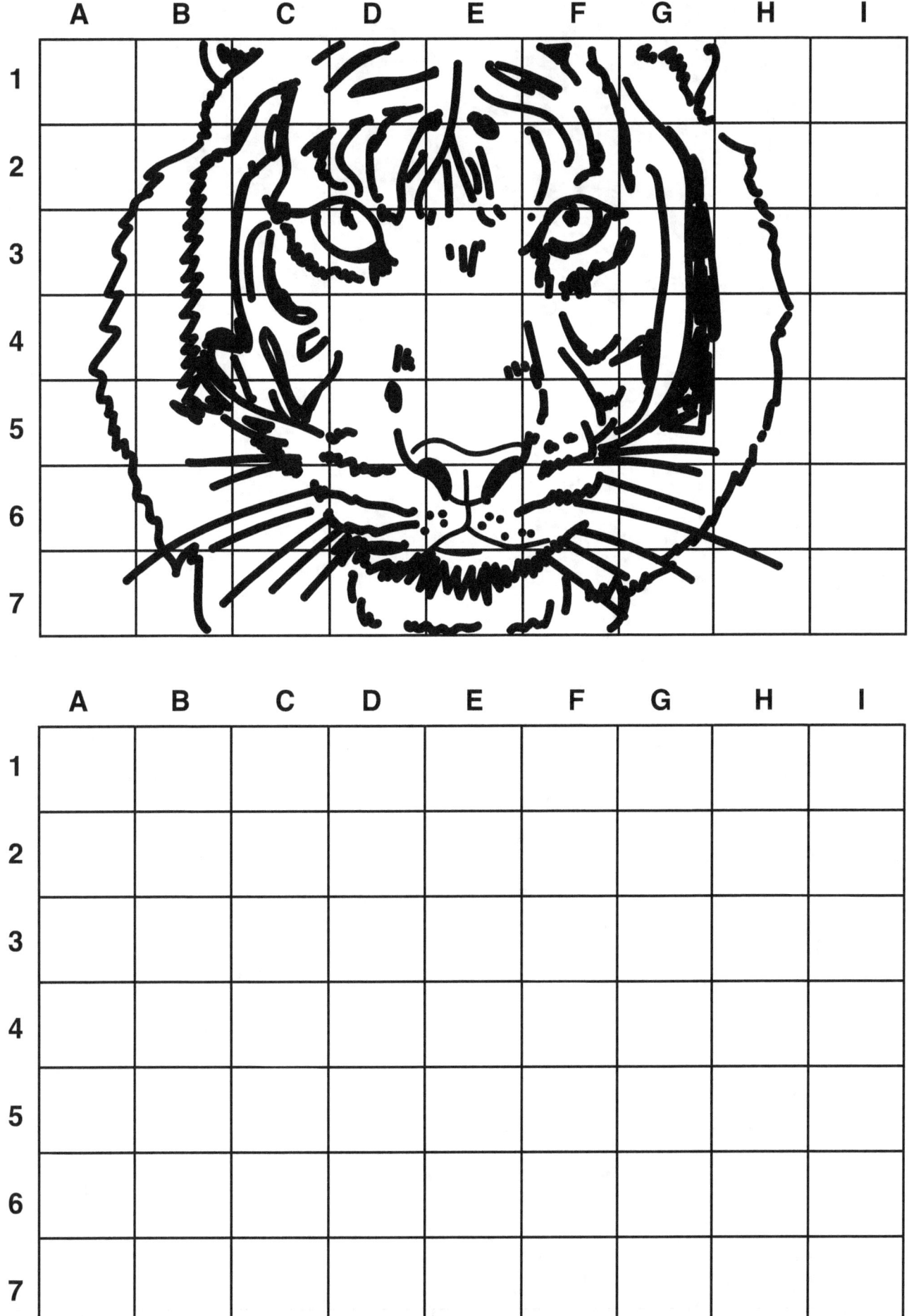

Messy Art Teacher 101 Grid Drawing Book I Page 45

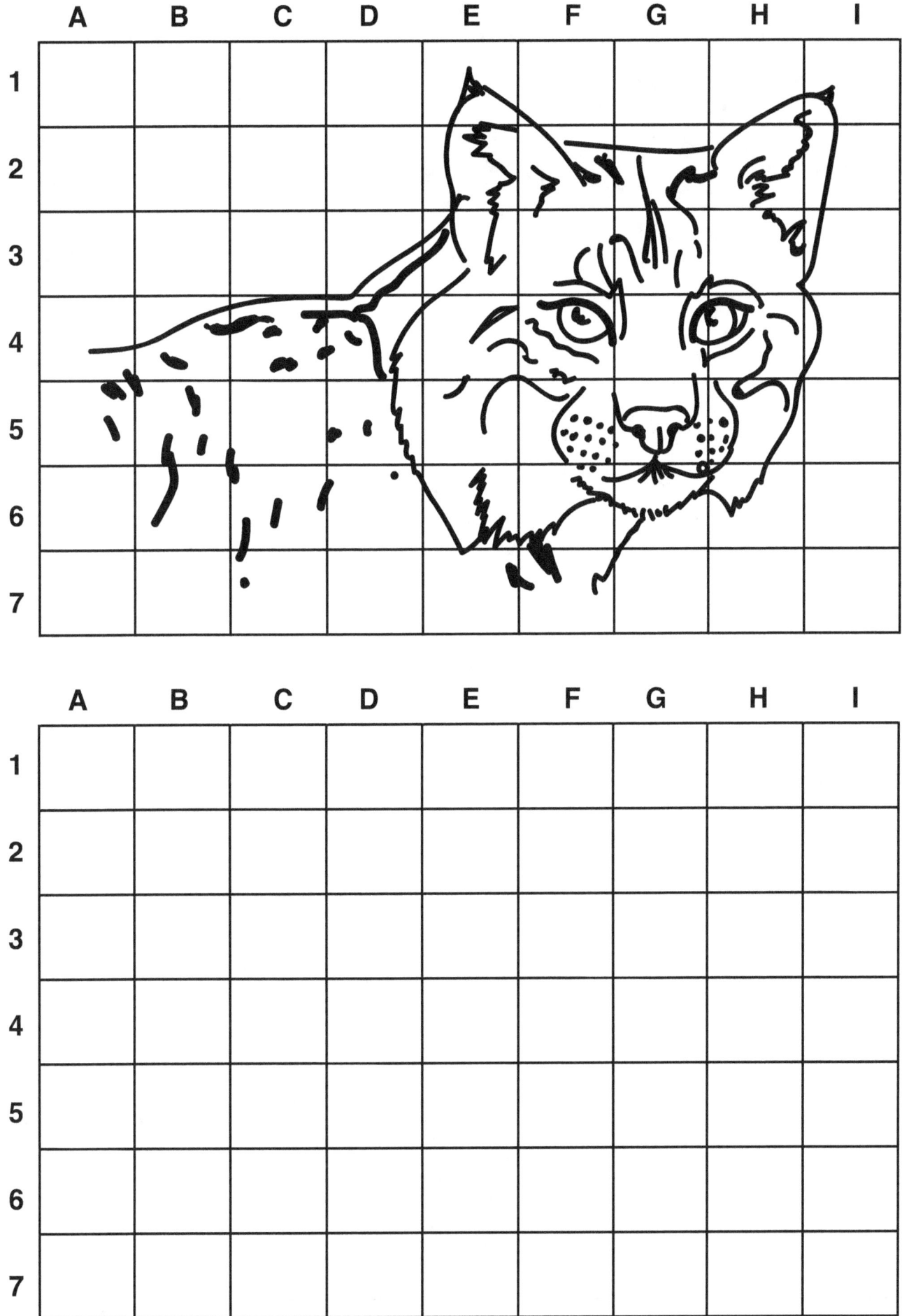

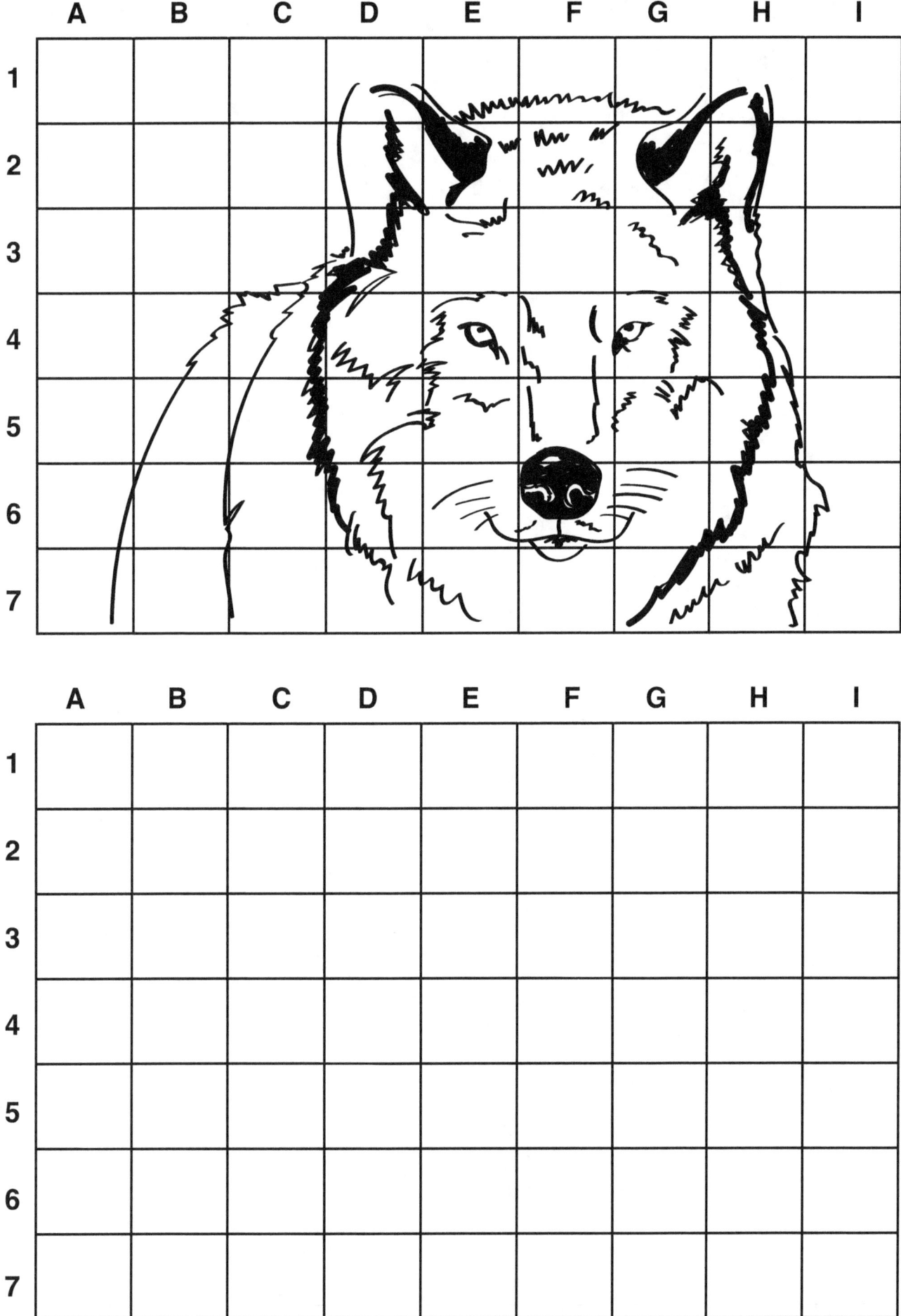

Copyright © 2020 by Messy Art Teacher. All rights reserved.

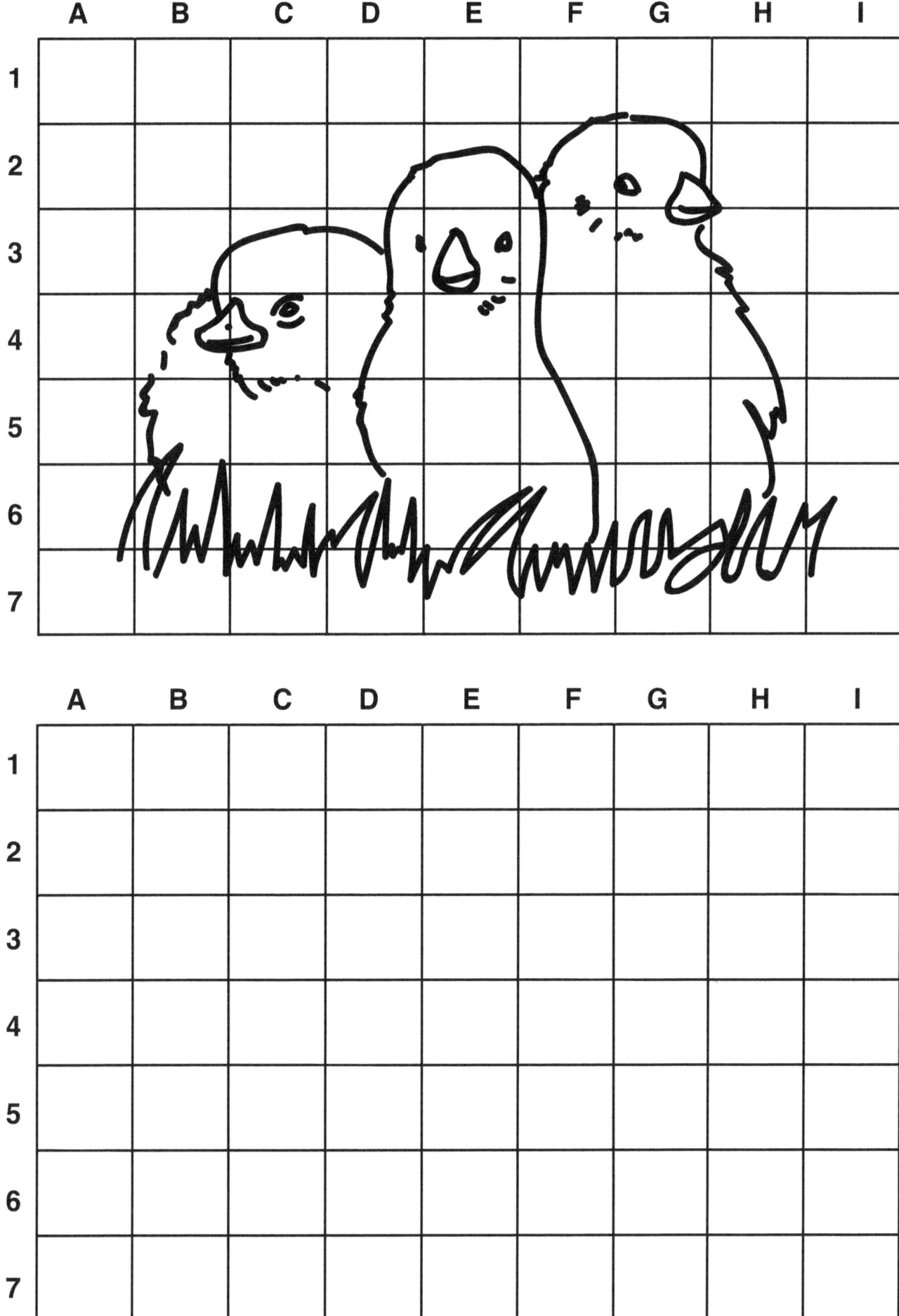

Messy Art Teacher 101 Grid Drawing Book I Page 51

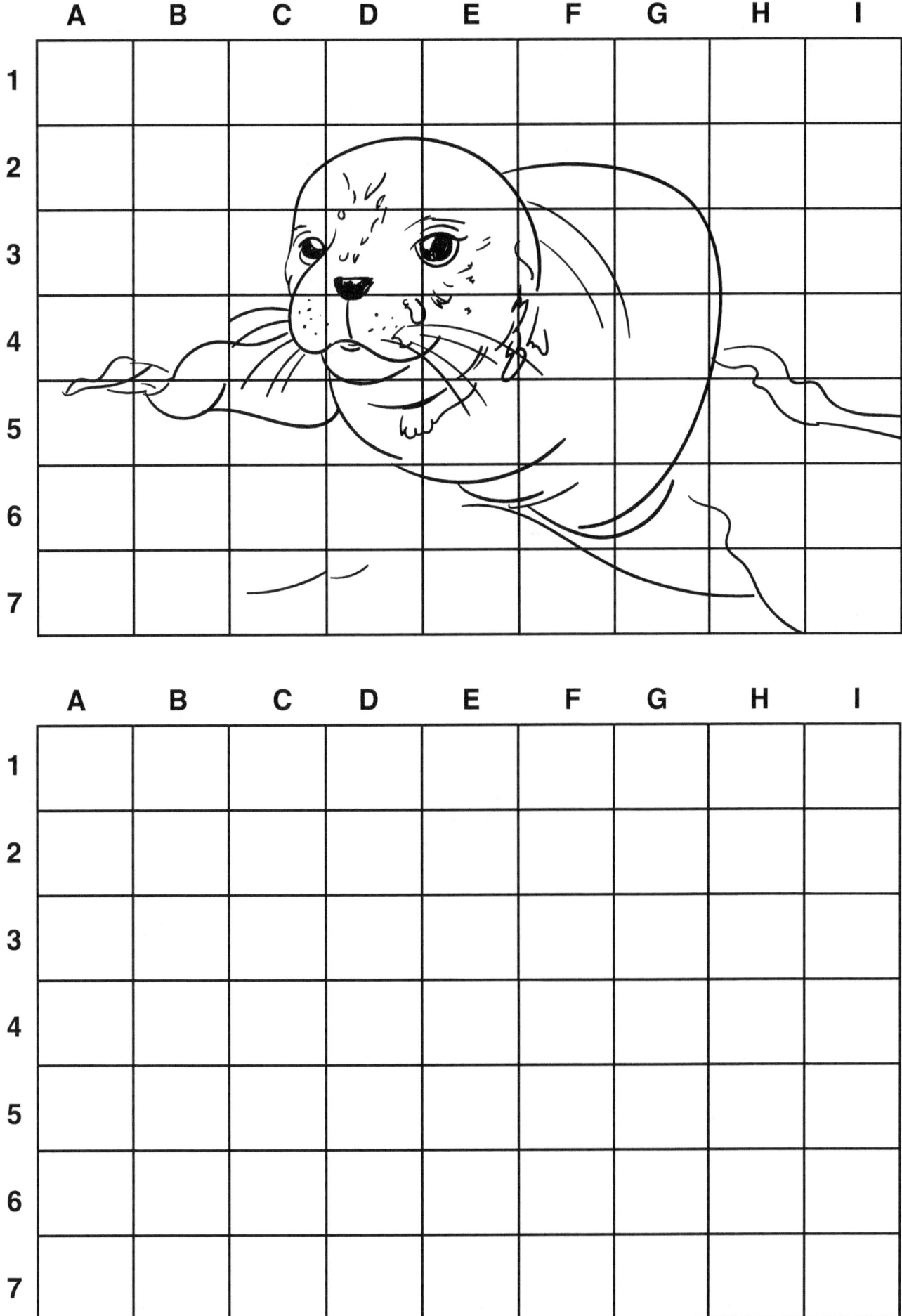

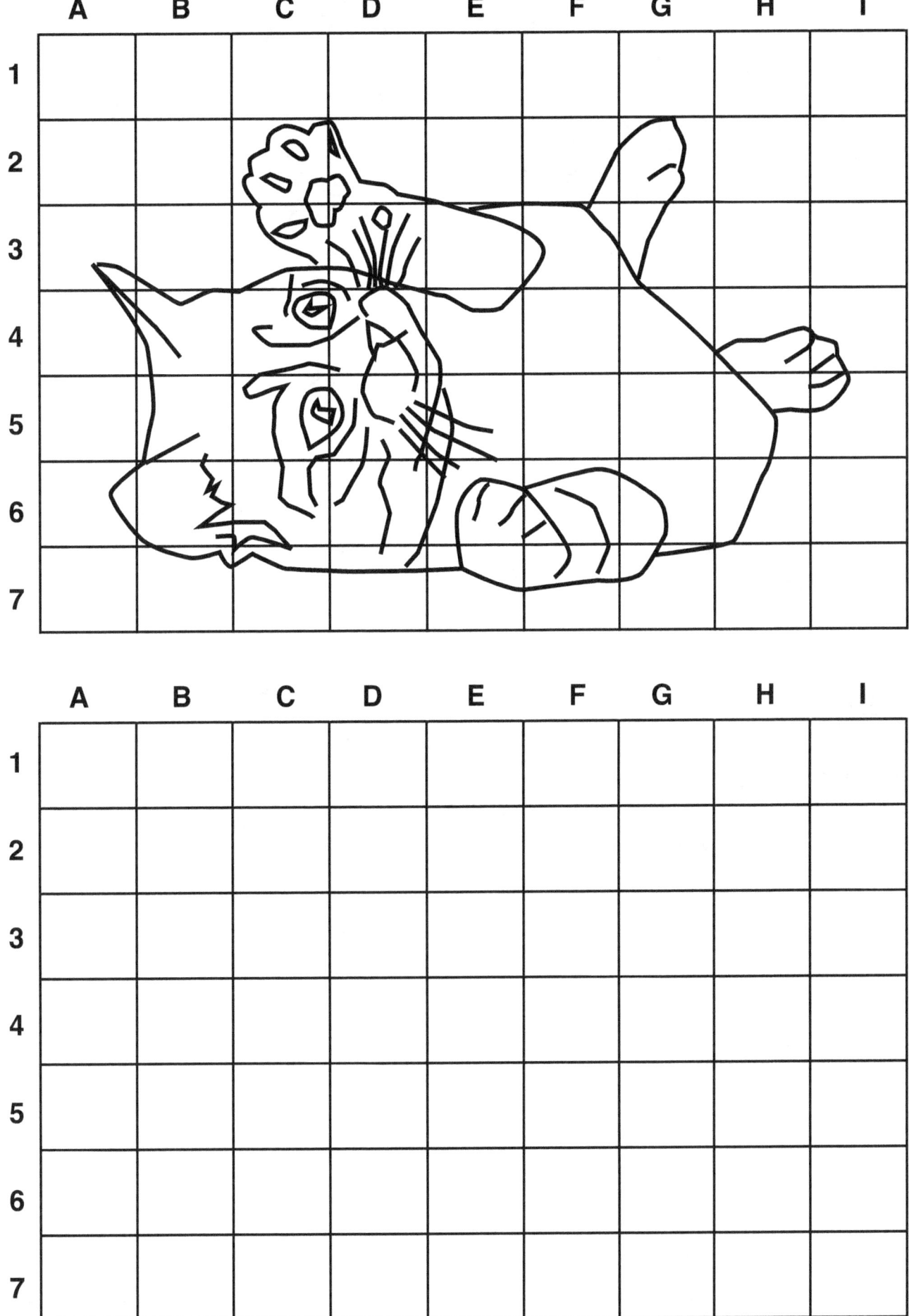

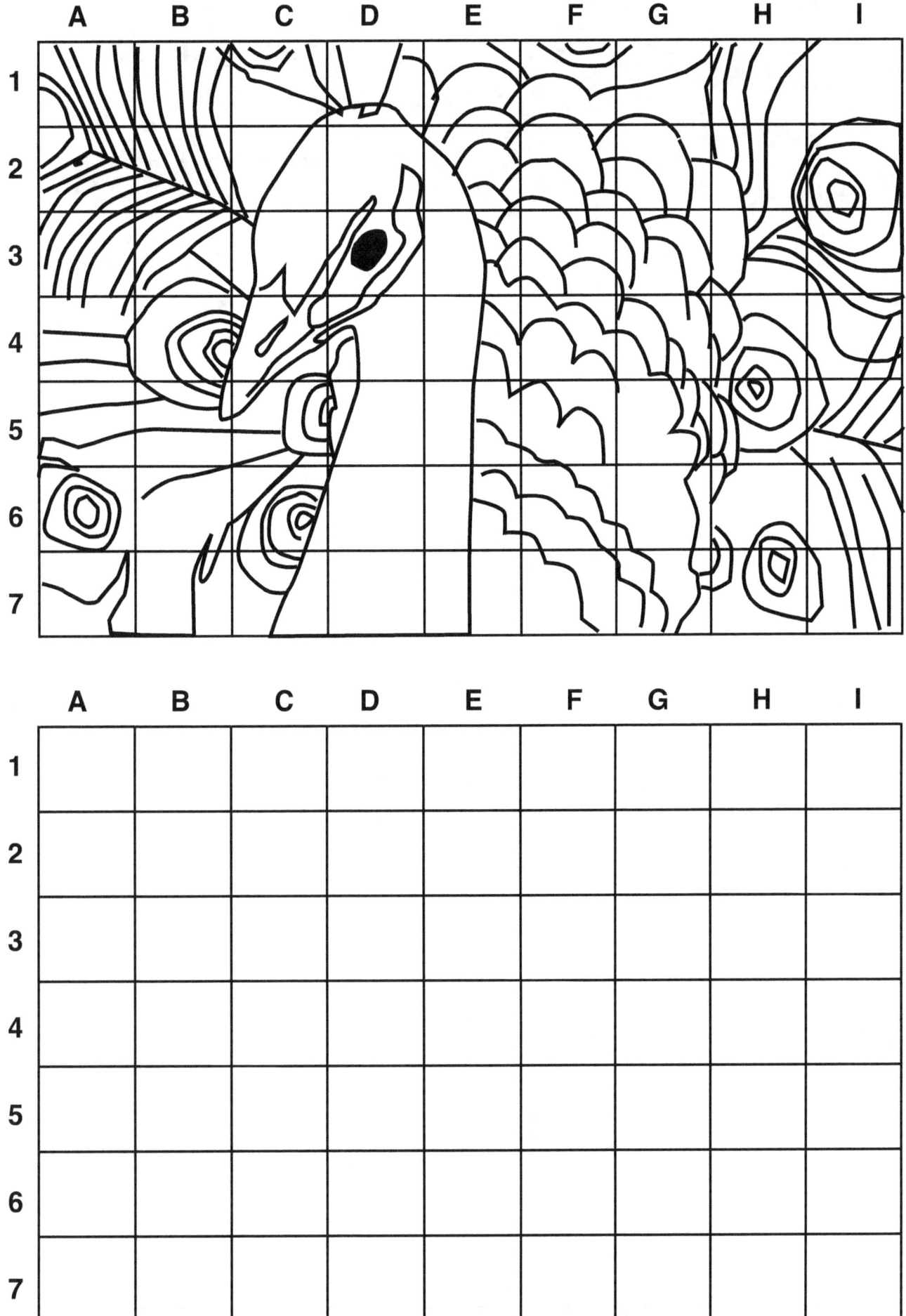

Messy Art Teacher 101 Grid Drawing Book | Page 57

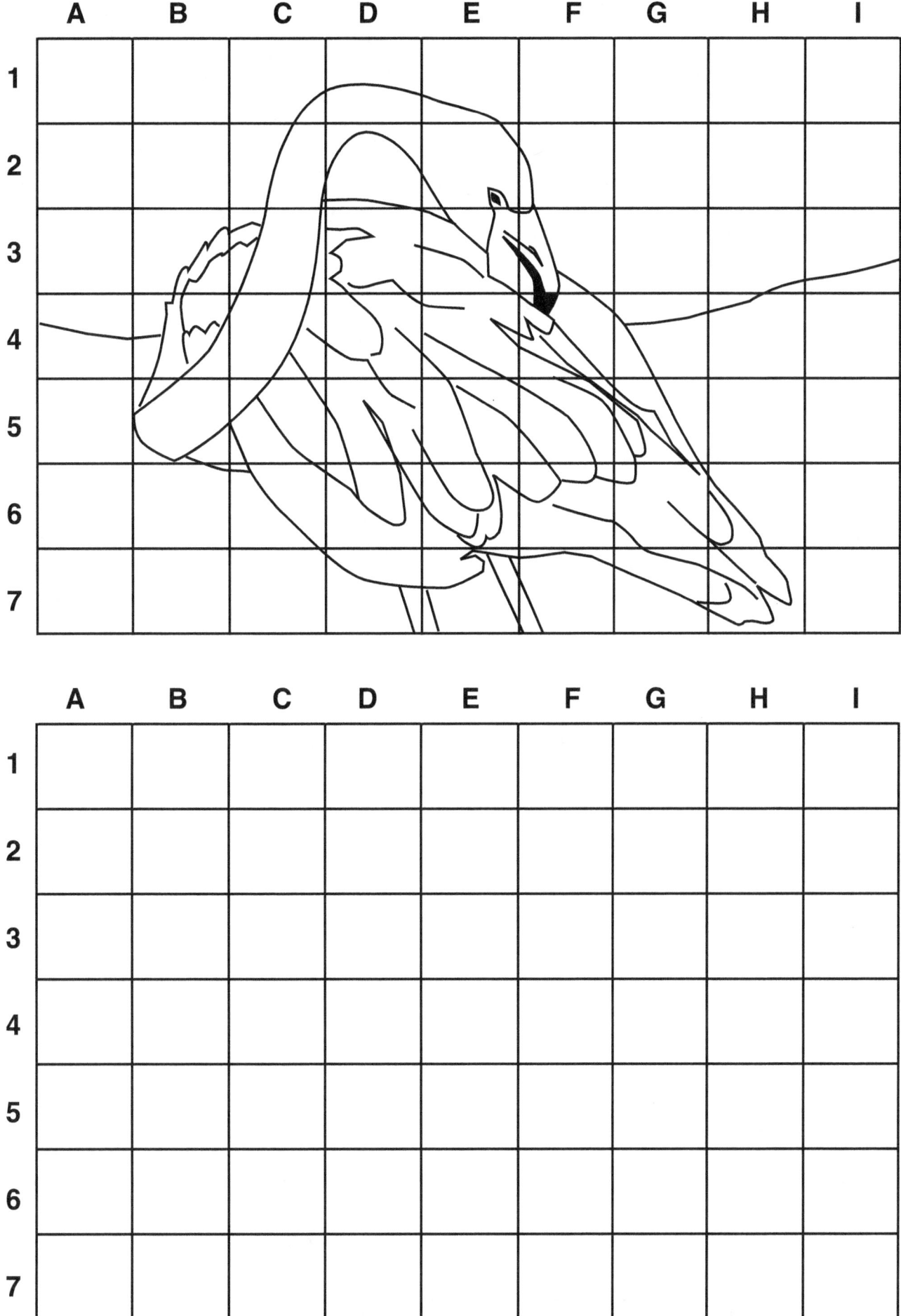

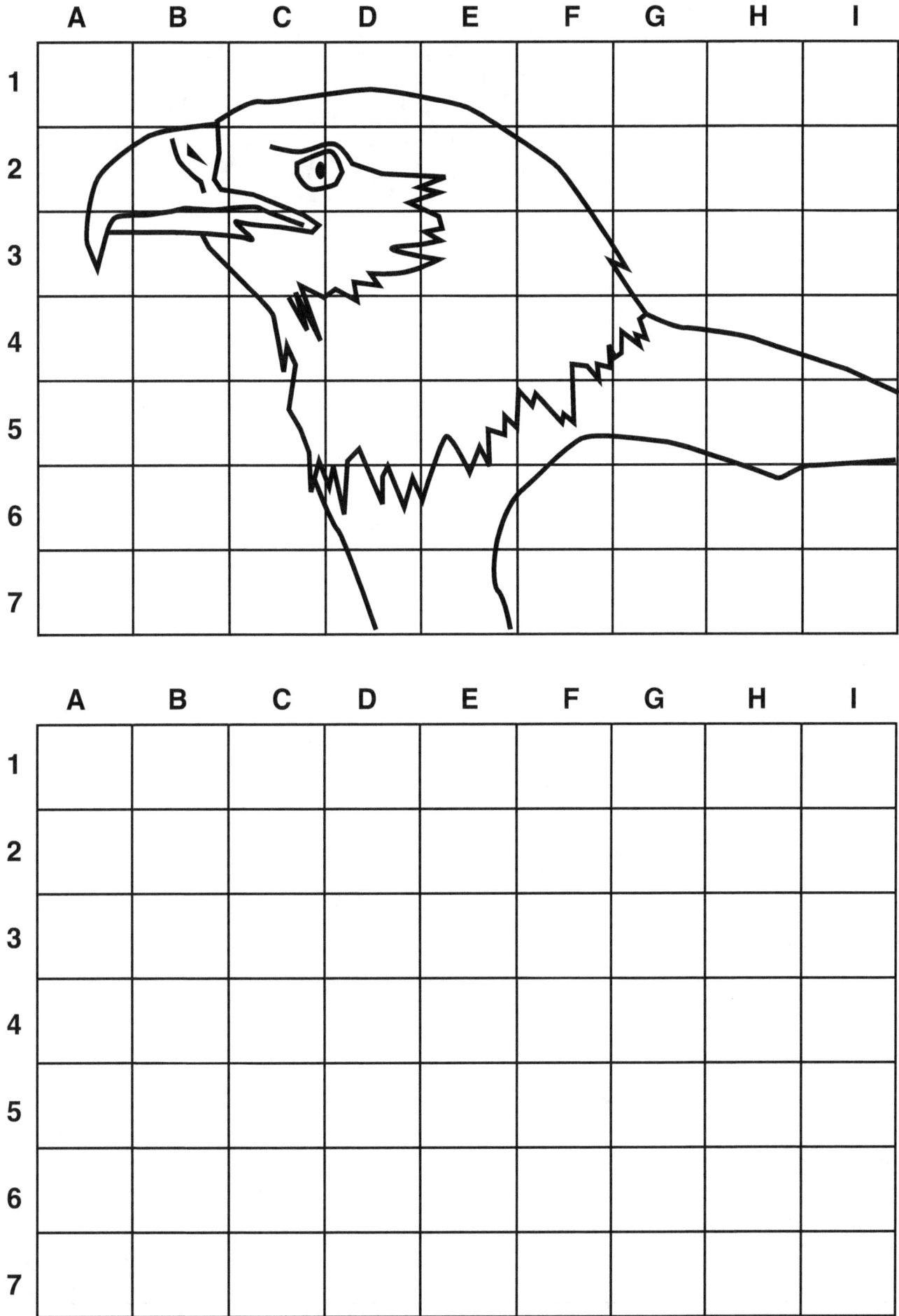

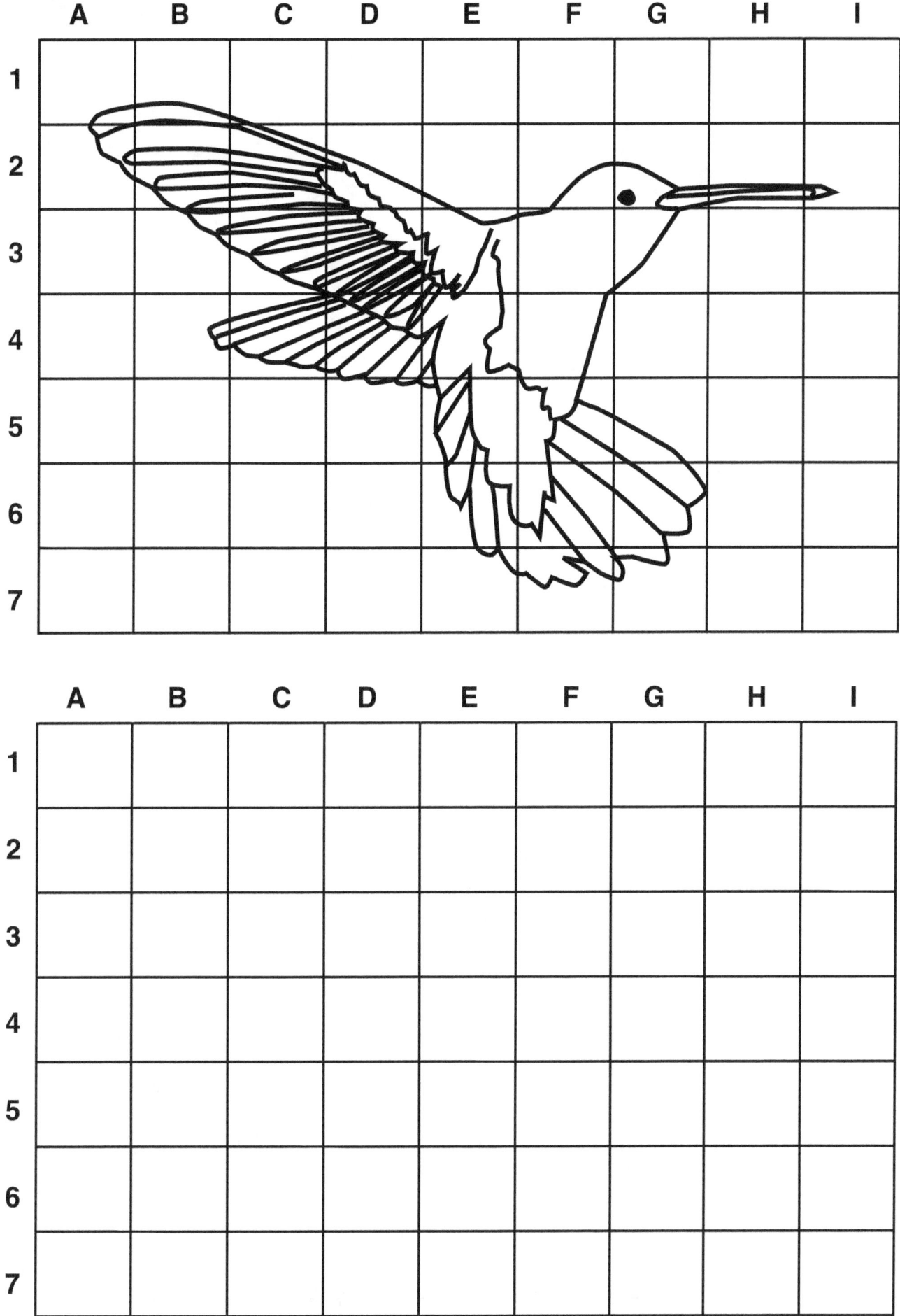

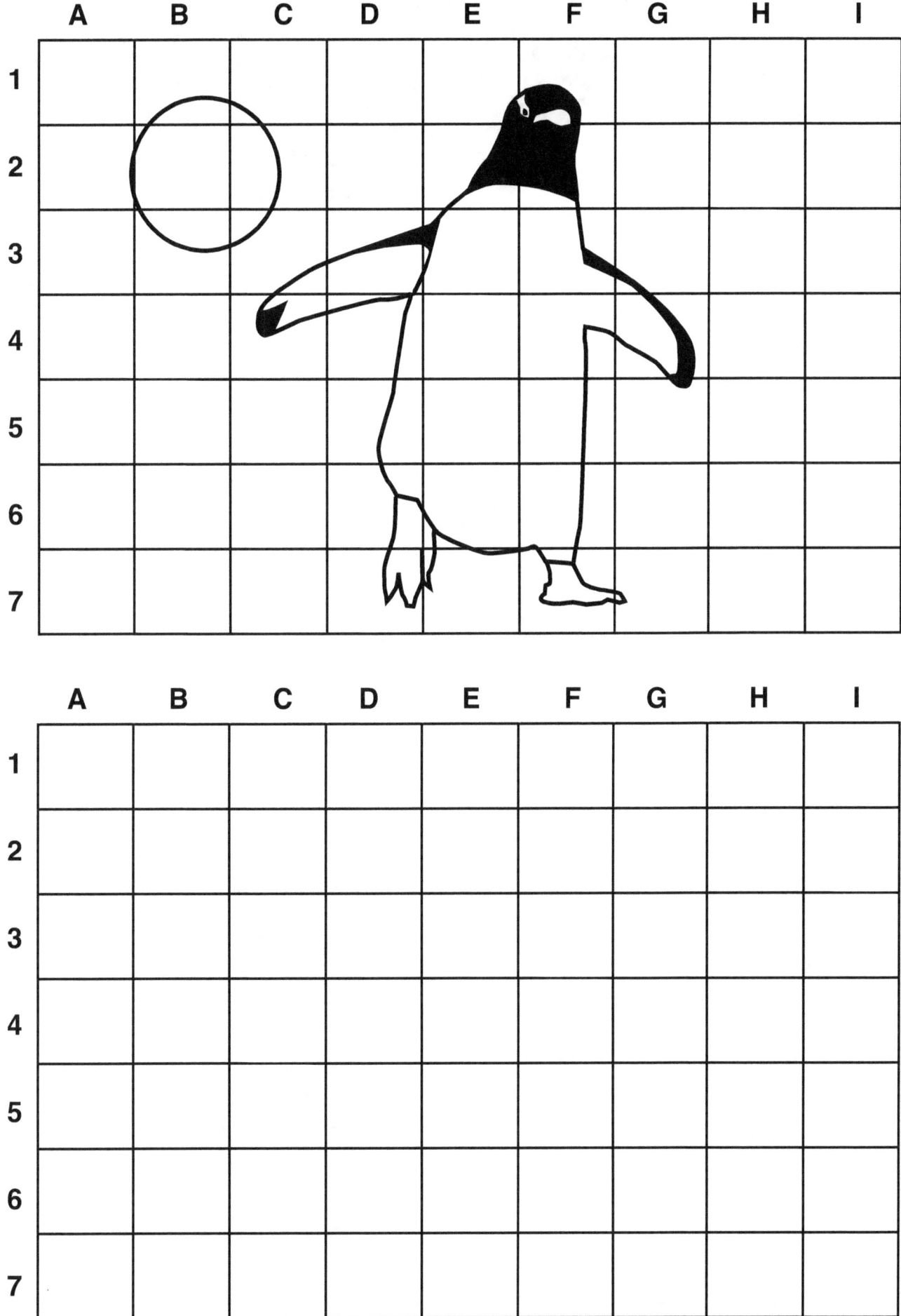

Copyright © 2020 by Messy Art Teacher. All rights reserved.

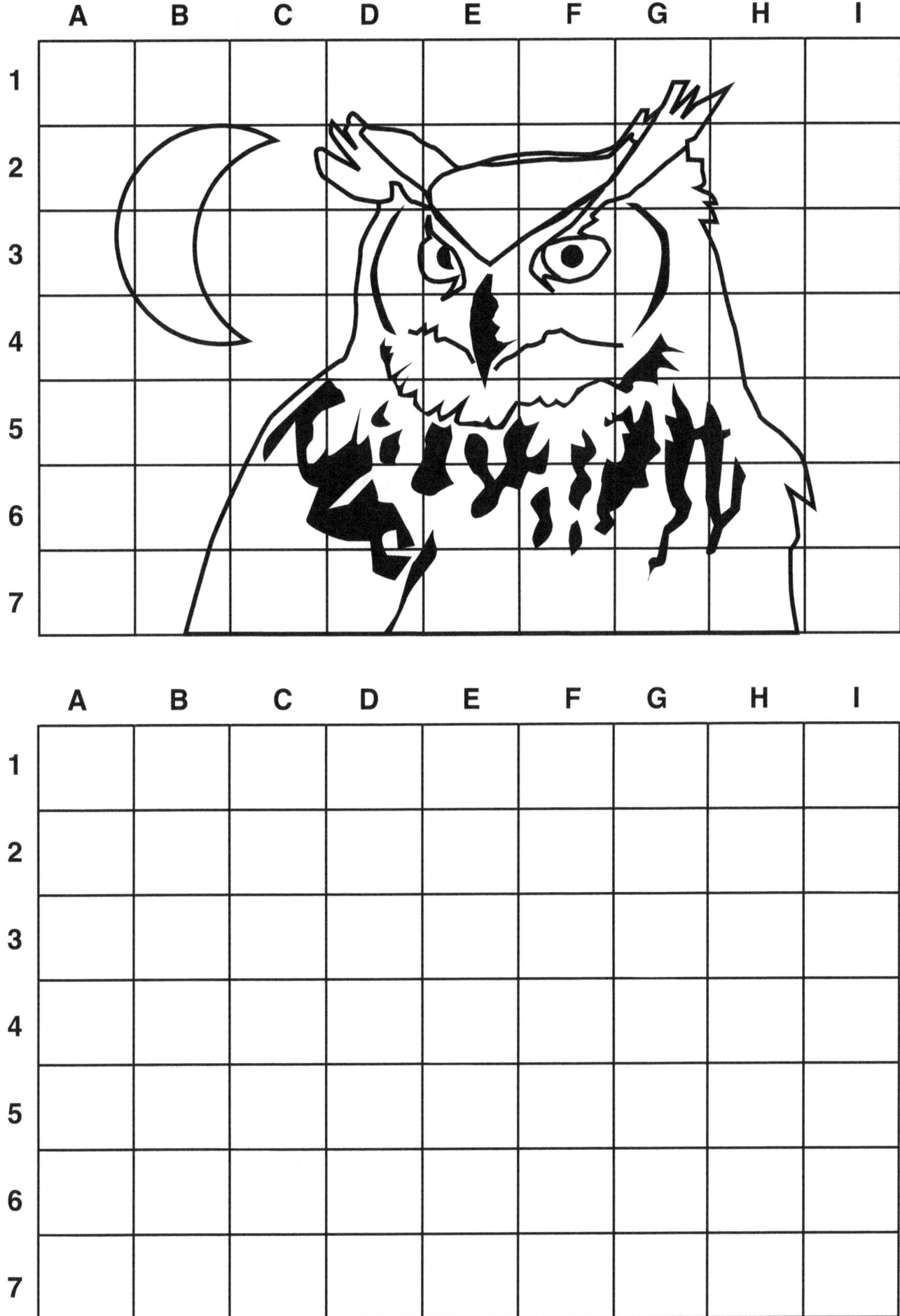

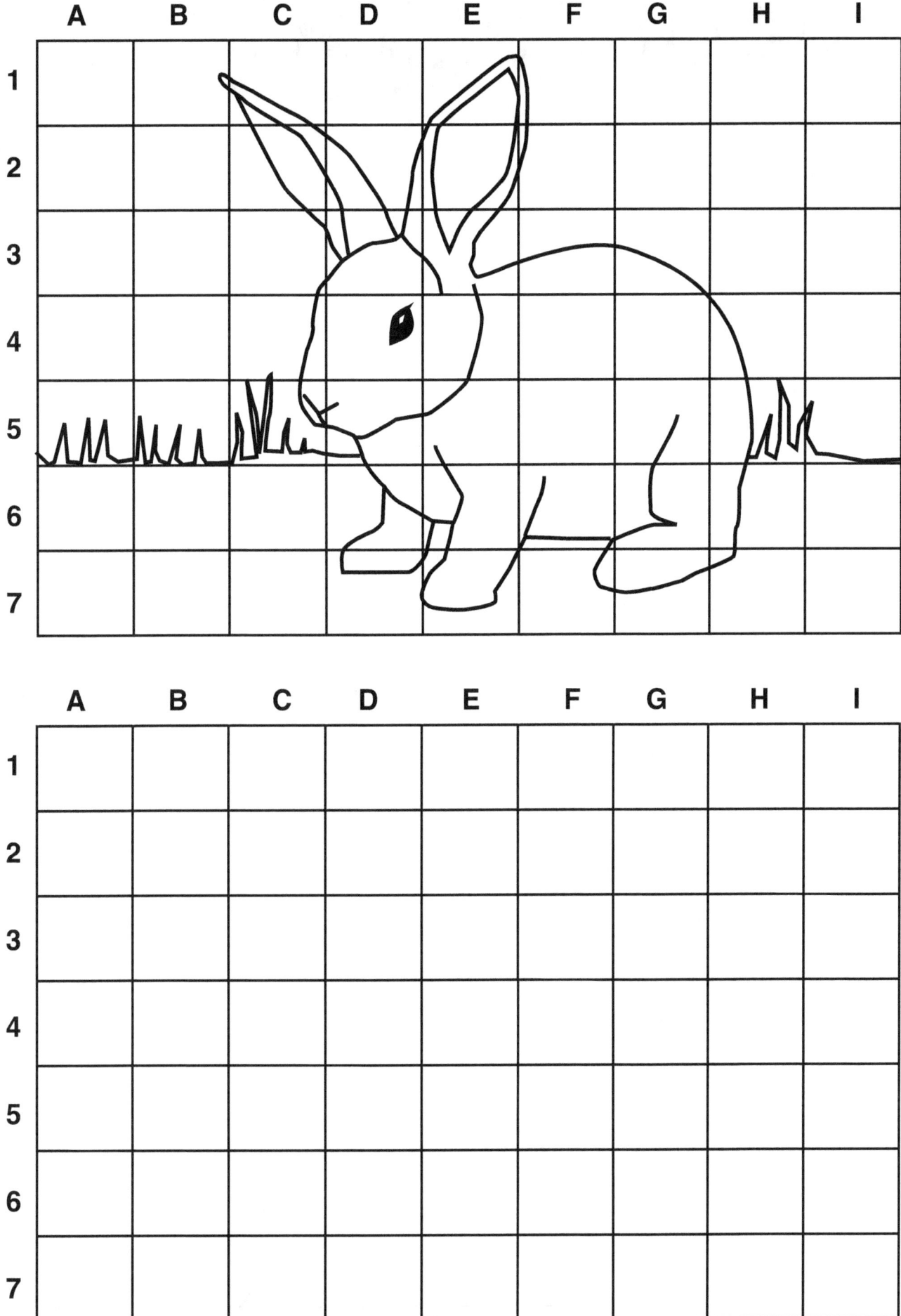

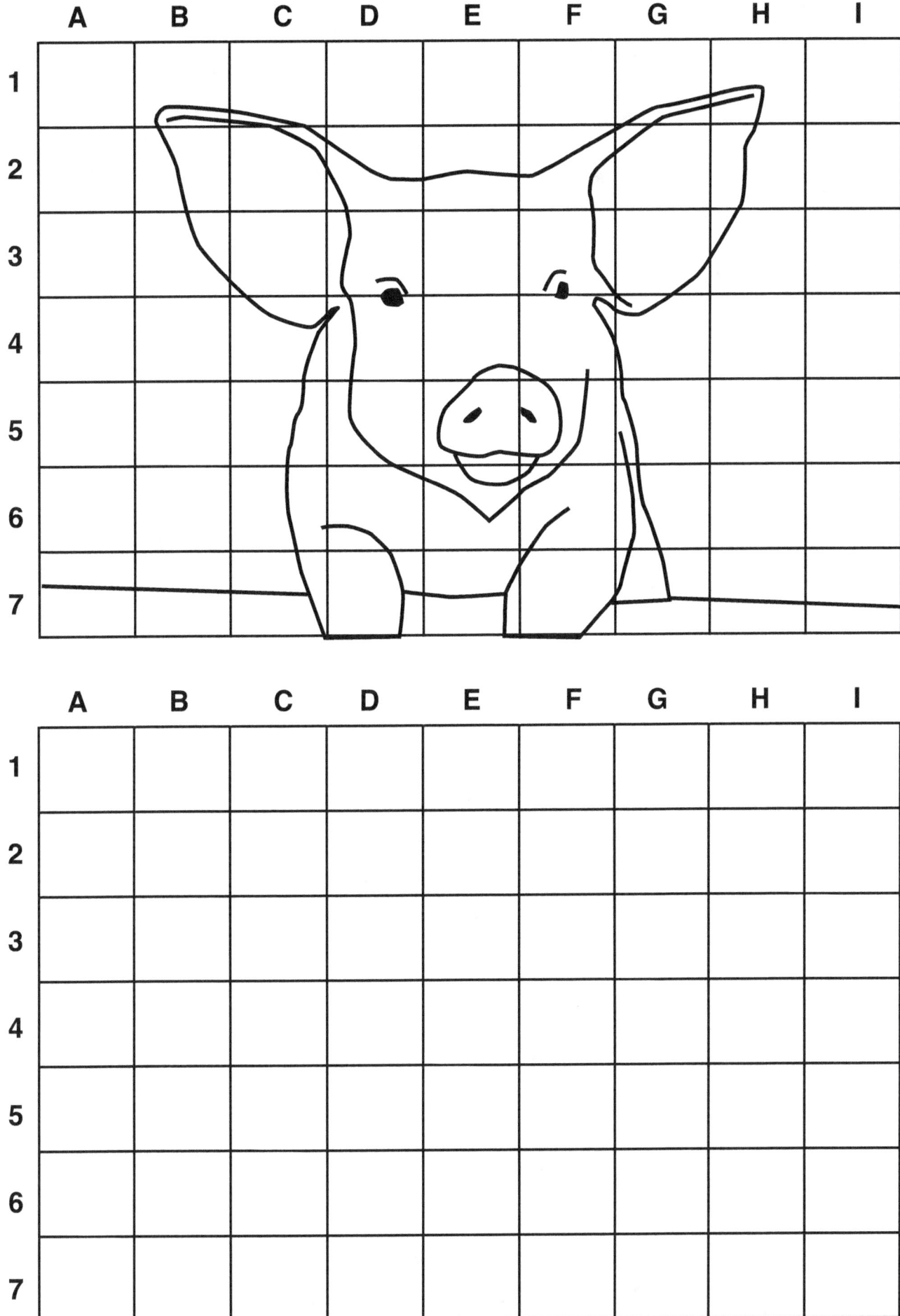

Messy Art Teacher 101 Grid Drawing Book l Page 71

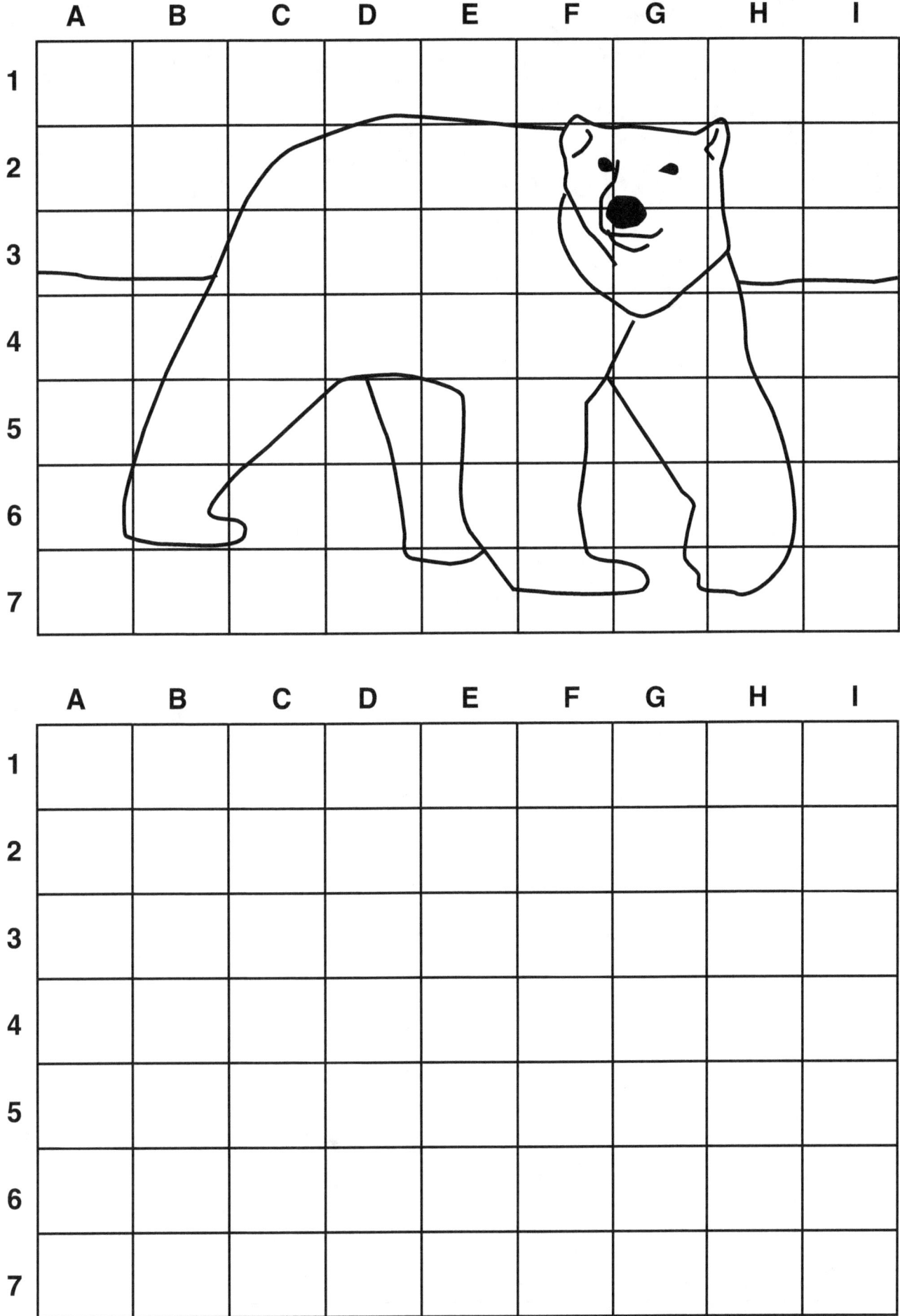

Copyright © 2020 by Messy Art Teacher. All rights reserved.

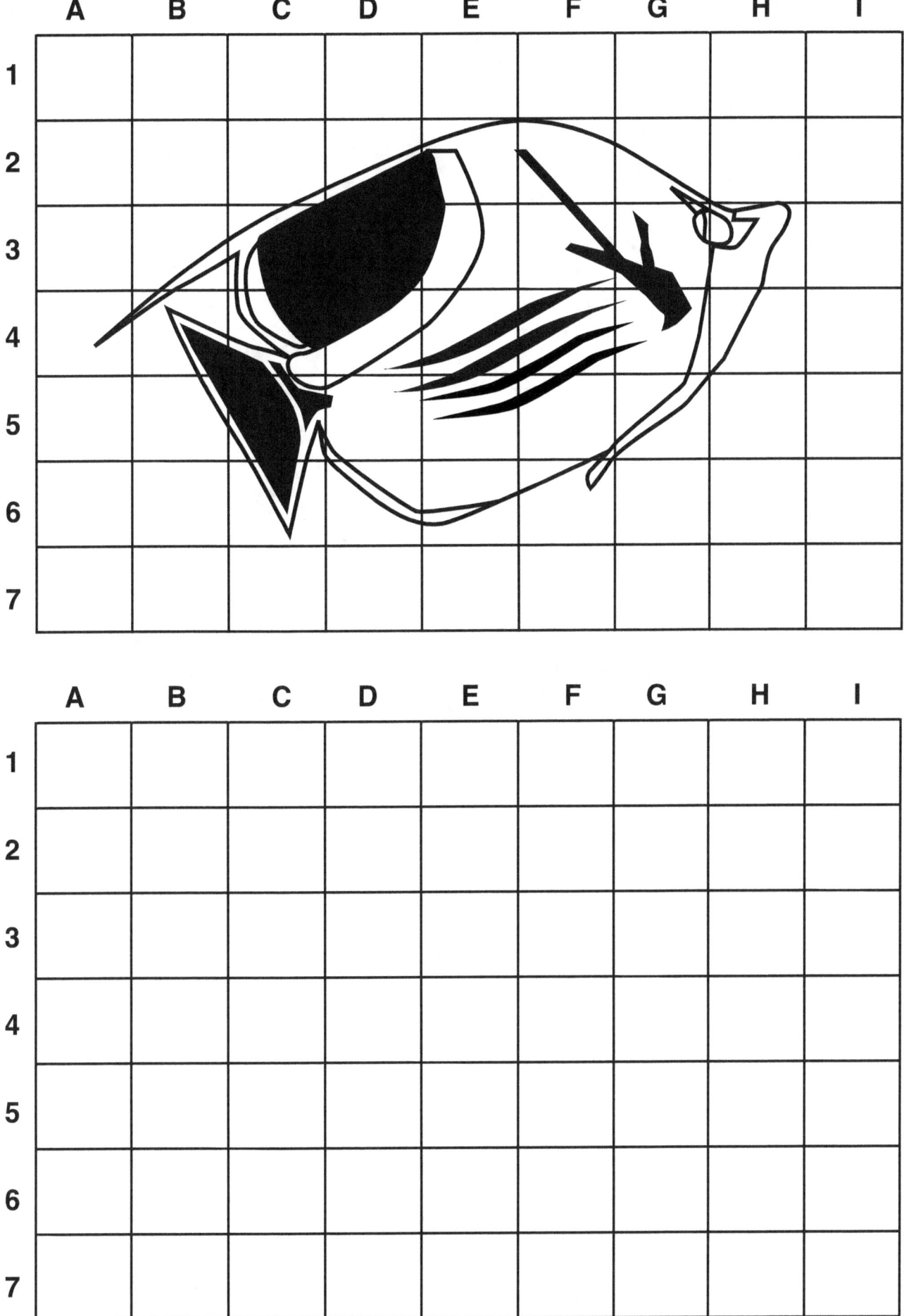

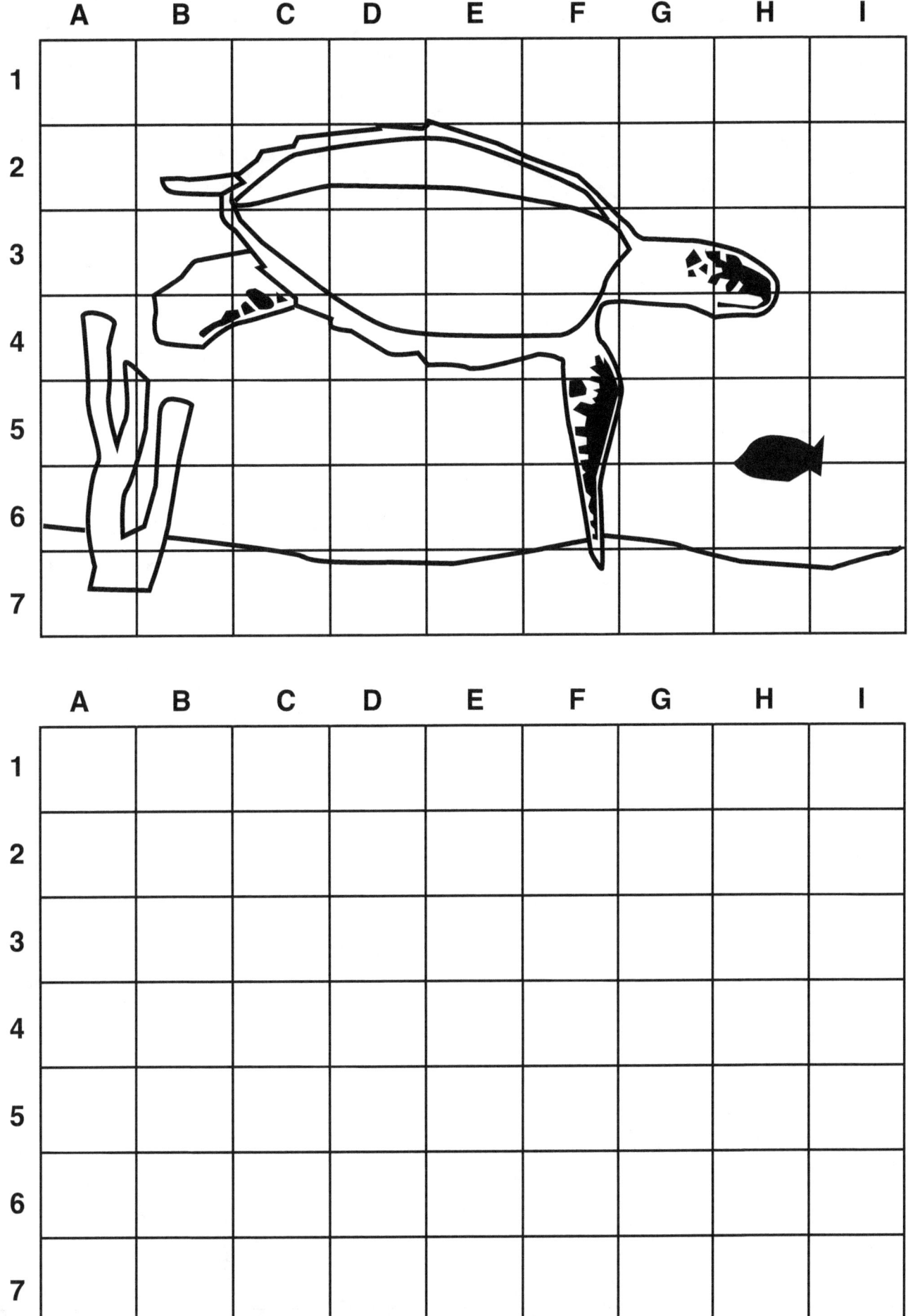

Messy Art Teacher 101 Grid Drawing Book | Page 77

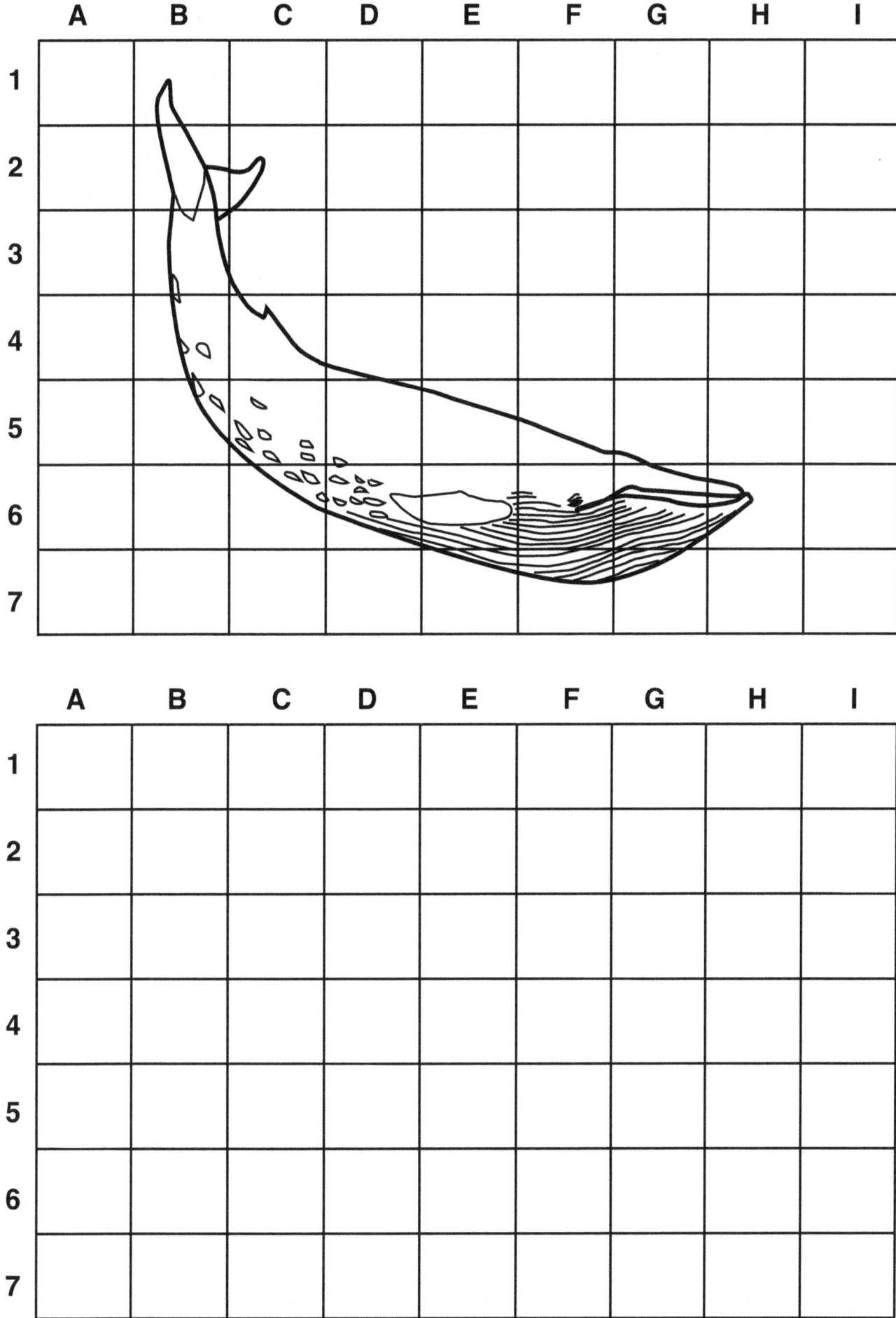

Messy Art Teacher 101 Grid Drawing Book | Page 79

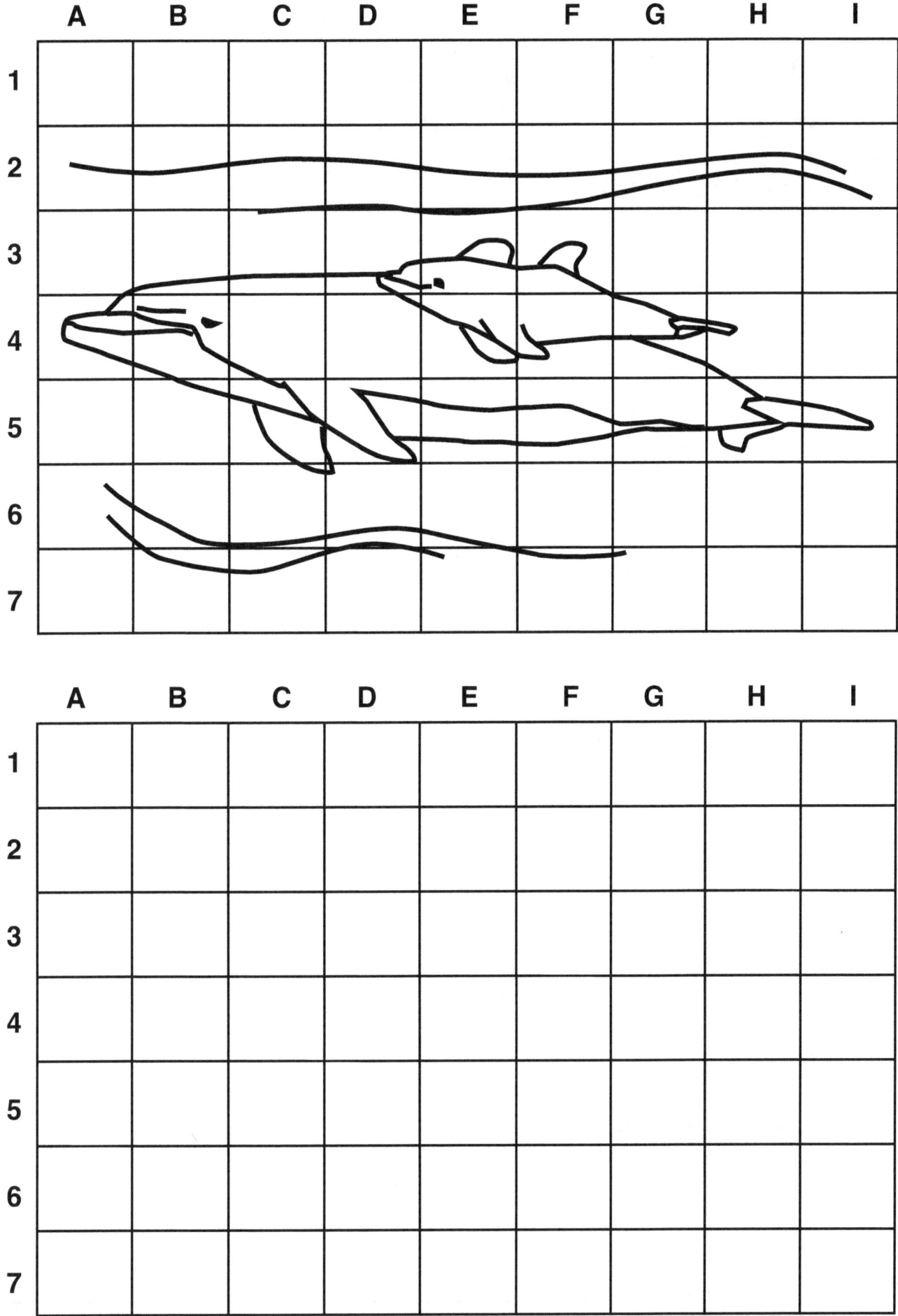

Messy Art Teacher 101 Grid Drawing Book | Page 81

Copyright © 2020 by Messy Art Teacher. All rights reserved.

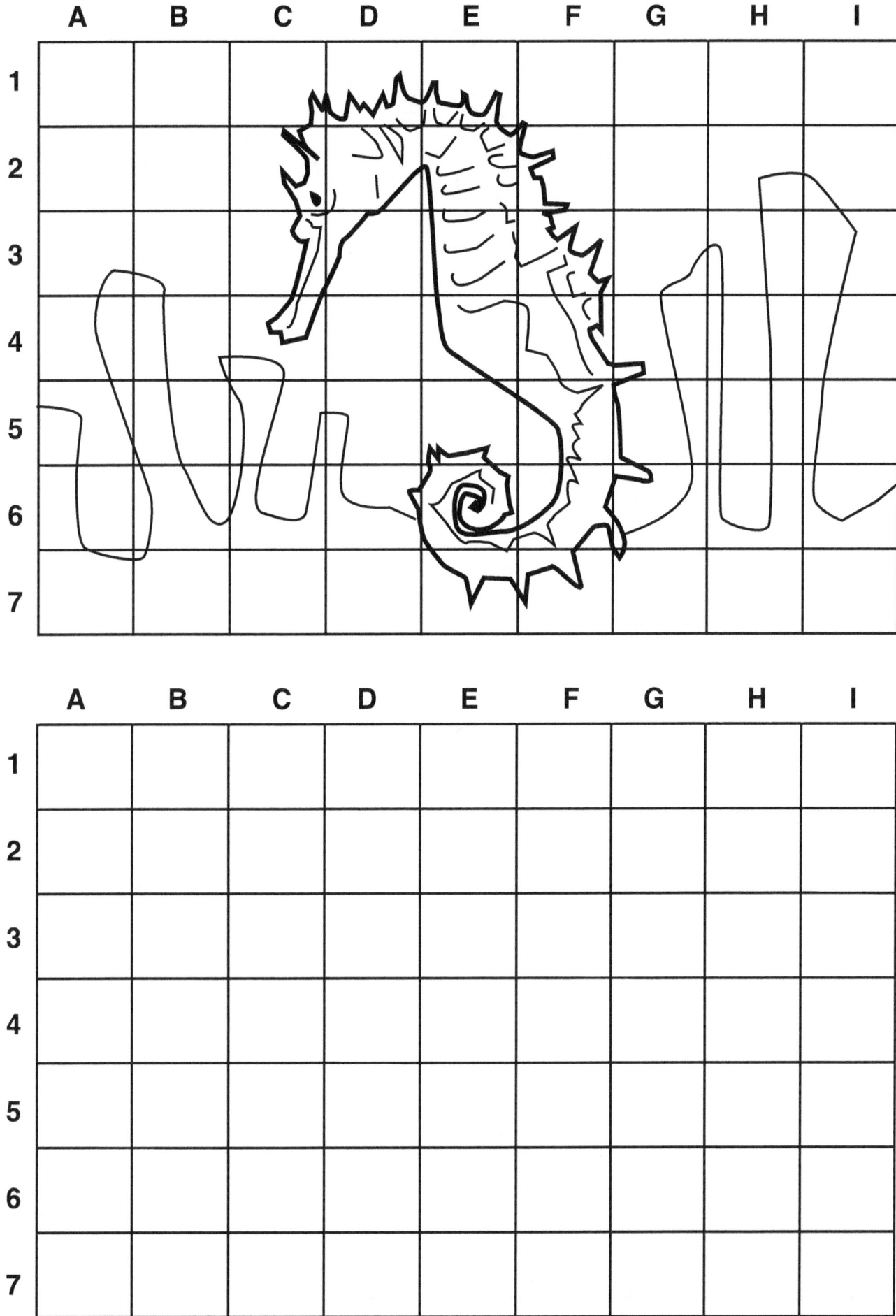

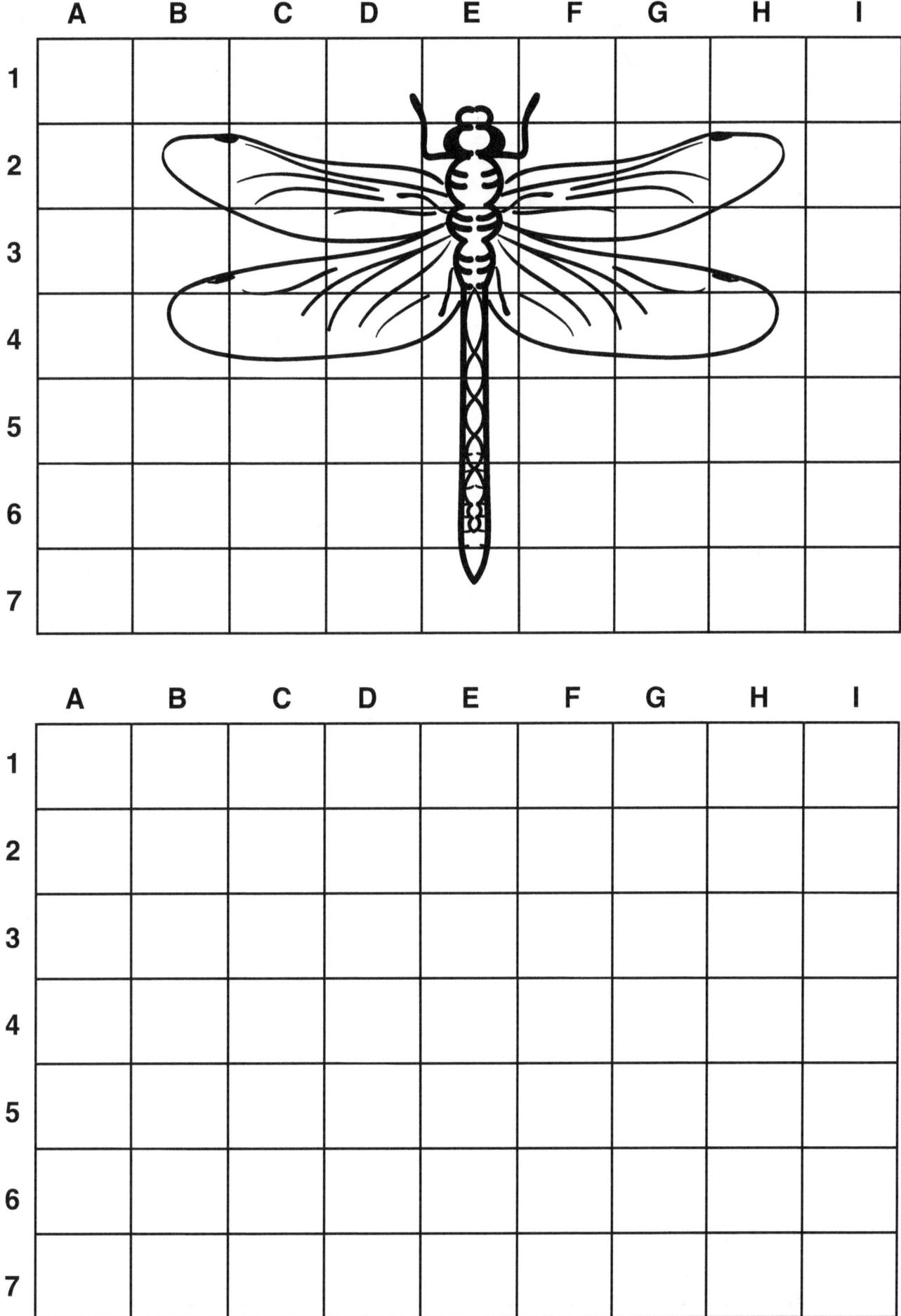

Messy Art Teacher 101 Grid Drawing Book I Page 85

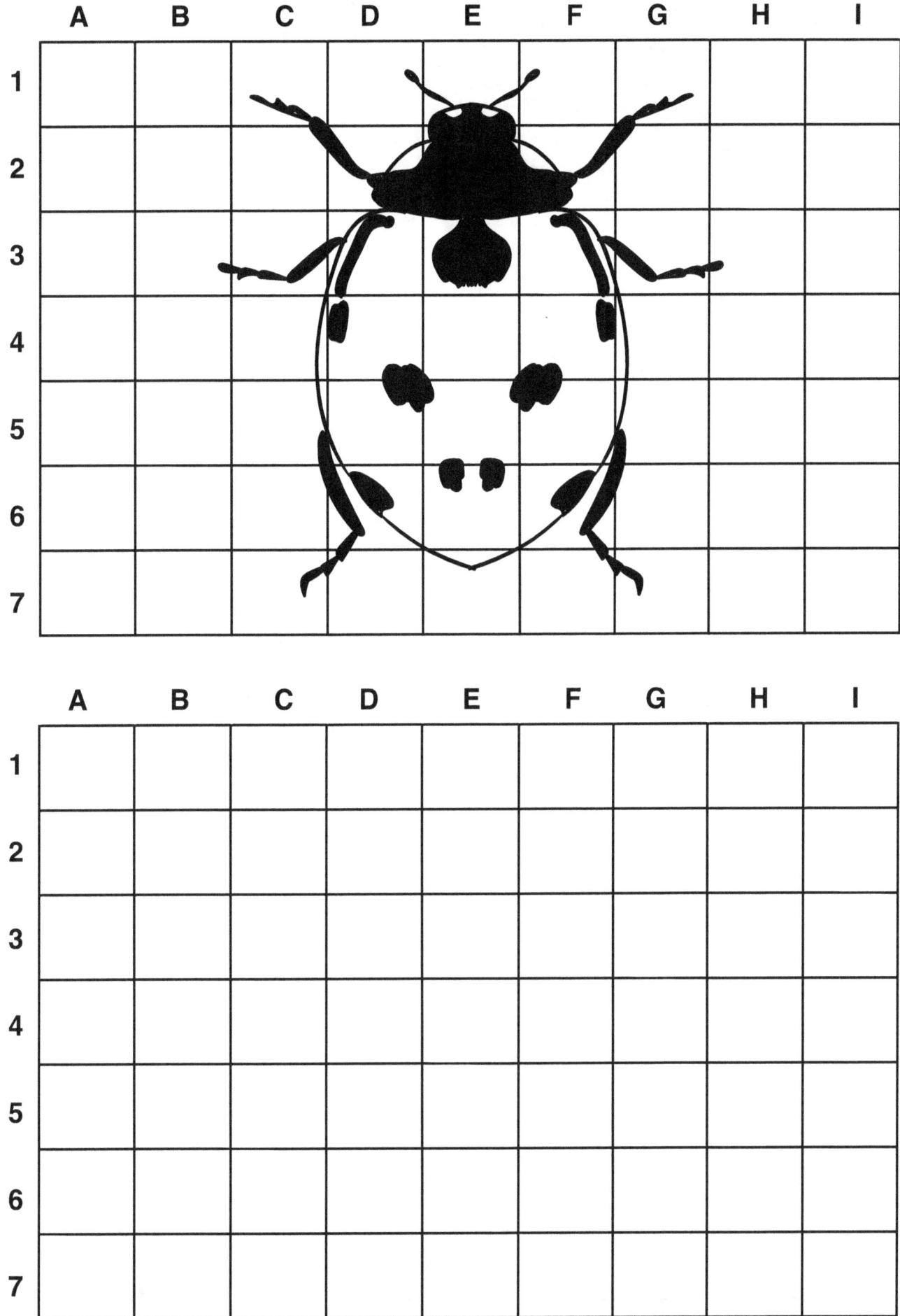

Copyright © 2020 by Messy Art Teacher. All rights reserved.

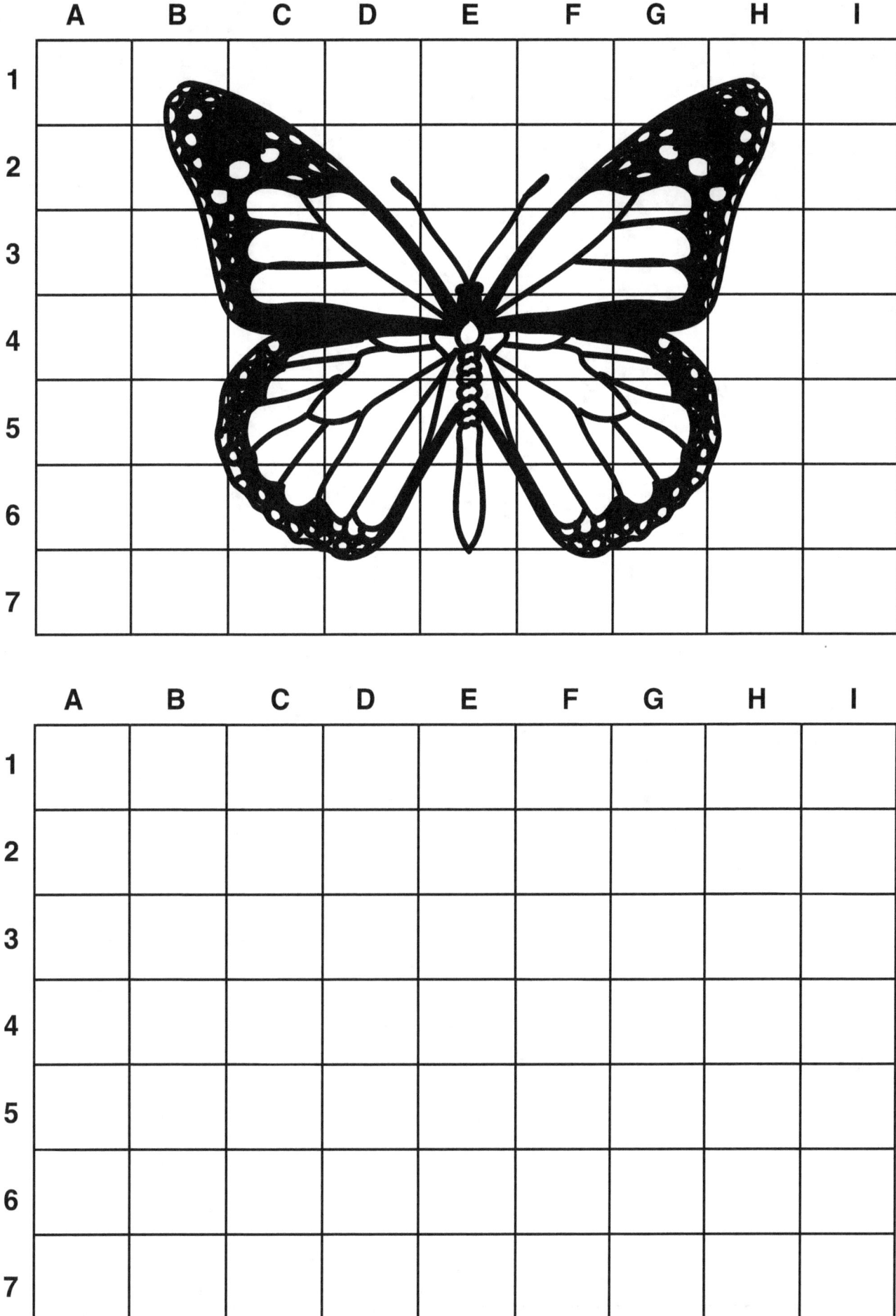

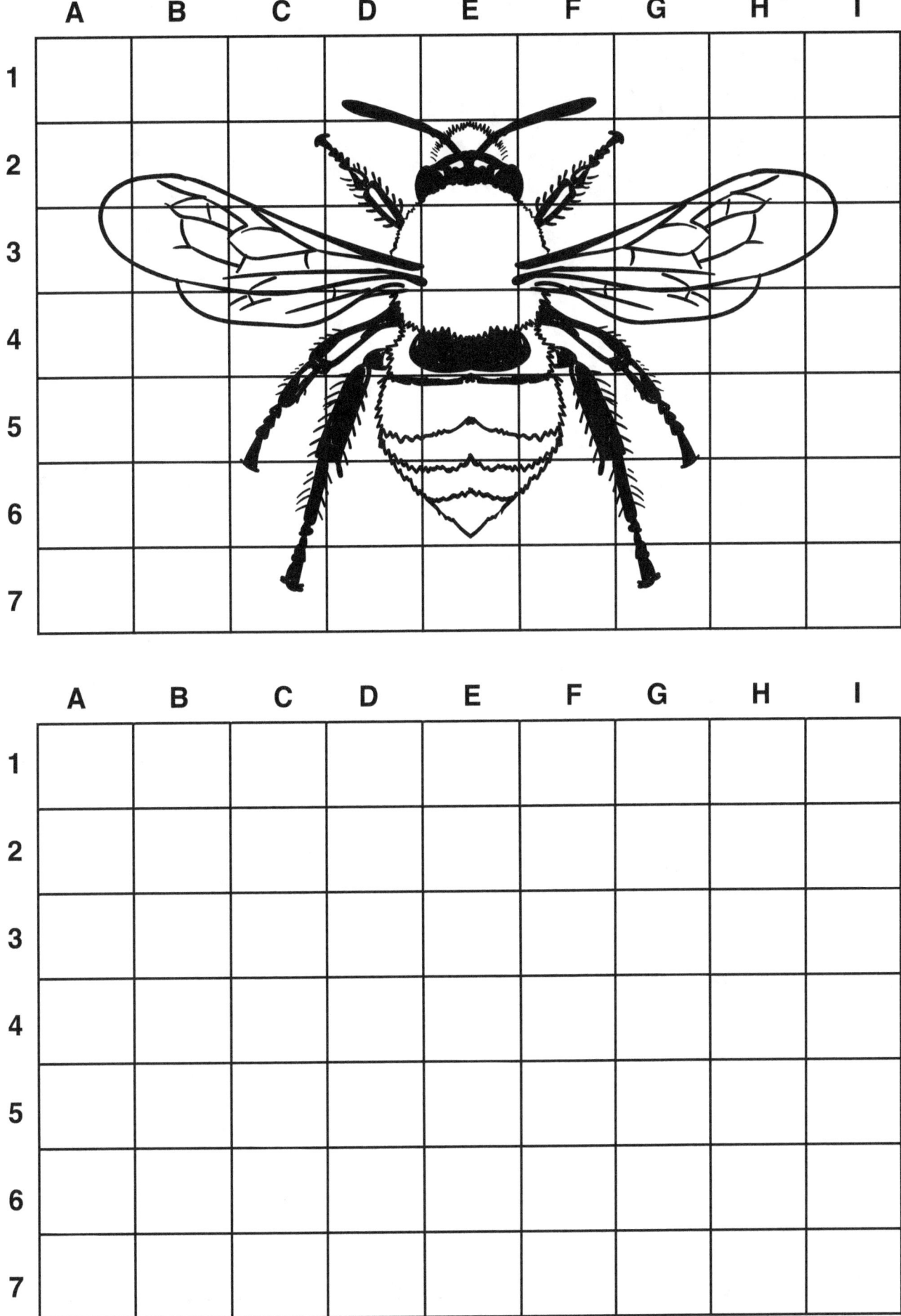

Messy Art Teacher 101 Grid Drawing Book | Page 91

	A	B	C	D	E	F	G	H	I
1									
2									
3									
4									
5									
6									
7									

	A	B	C	D	E	F	G	H	I
1									
2									
3									
4									
5									
6									
7